Ethics and Politics
in School Leadership

The Concordia University Chicago Leadership Series

An Educational Series from Rowman & Littlefield

Series Editor: Daniel R. Tomal

Education leaders have many titles and positions in American schools today: professors, K-12 teachers, district and building administrators, teacher coaches, teacher evaluators, directors, coordinators, staff specialists, etc. More than ever, educators need practical and proven educational and leadership resources to stay current and advance the learning of students.

The Concordia University Chicago Leadership Series is a unique resource that addresses this need. The authors of this series are award-winning authors and scholars who are both passionate theorists and practitioners of this valuable collection of works. They give realistic and real-life examples and strategies to help all educators inspire and make a difference in school improvement and student learning that gets results.

This Leadership Series consists of a variety of distinctive books on subjects of school change, research, completing advanced degrees, school administration, leadership and motivation, business finance and resources, human resource management, challenging students to learn, action research for practitioners, the teacher as a coach, school law and policies, ethics, and many other topics that are critical to modern educators in meeting the emerging and diverse students of today. These books also align with current federal, state, and various association accreditation standards and elements.

Staying current and building the future require the knowledge and strategies presented in these books. The Leadership Series Originator, Daniel R. Tomal, PhD, is an award-winning author who has published over 19 books and 200 articles and studies, and is a highly sought-after speaker and educational researcher. He, along with his coauthors, provides a wealth of educational experience, proven strategies that can help all educators aspire to be the best they can be in meeting the demands of modern educational leadership.

Titles in the Series

Grant Writing: Strategies for Scholars and Professionals
Supervision and Evaluation for Learning and Growth
The Teacher Leader: Core Competencies and Strategies for Effective Leadership
How to Finish and Defend Your Dissertation: Strategies to Complete the Professional Practice Doctorate
Leading School Change: Maximizing Resources for School Improvement
Managing Human Resources and Collective Bargaining
Resource Management for School Administrators: Optimizing Fiscal, Facility, and Human Resources
Action Research for Educators—Second Edition
Challenging Students to Learn: How to Use Effective Leadership and Motivation Tactics
Action Research for Educators
Discipline by Negotiation: Methods for Managing Student Behavior
Technology for Classroom and Online Learning: An Educator's Guide to Bits, Bytes, and Teaching
The Challenge for School Leaders: A New Way of Thinking About Leadership

Ethics and Politics in School Leadership

Finding Common Ground

Jeffrey T. Brierton, Brenda F. Graham, Daniel R. Tomal, and Robert K. Wilhite

ROWMAN & LITTLEFIELD
Lanham • Boulder • New York • London

Published by Rowman & Littlefield
A wholly owned subsidary of The Rowman & Littlefield Publishing Group, Inc.
4501 Forbes Boulevard, Suite 200, Lanham, Maryland 20706
www.rowman.com

Unit A, Whitacre Mews, 26-34 Stannary Street, London SE11 4AB

British Library Cataloguing in Publication Information Available

Library of Congress Cataloging-in-Publication Data

Names: Brierton, Jeffrey T.
Title: Ethics and politics in school leadership : finding common ground / edited by
    Jeffrey T. Brierton, Brenda F. Graham, and Daniel R. Tomal.
Description: Lanham, Maryland : Rowman & Littlefield, 2016. I Series: Concordia
    University Chicago Leadership series I Includes bibliographical references and index.
Identifiers: LCCN 2015041044I ISBN 9781475818987 (cloth : alk. paper) I
    ISBN 9781475818994 (pbk. : alk. paper) I ISBN 9781475819007 (electronic)
Subjects: LCSH: School administrators—Professional ethics. I Educational
    leadership—Moral and ethical aspects. I School management and organization—
    Moral and ethical aspects.
Classification: LCC LB1779 .E7385 2016 I DDC 371.2—dc23 LC record available at
    http://lccn.loc.gov/2015041044

Printed in the United States of America

In appreciation to all the graduate students of Concordia University Chicago, who have chosen the path to leadership, along with the dedicated faculty who guide them on their journey. Our schools need you more than ever, and may you always lead from the front.

Praise for *Ethics and Politics in School Leadership*

"The book is a must-read for all people connected with education. It deals with two very important topics—ethics and leadership—and explains them in a way that brings clarity and purpose to a very important subject. I strongly recommend this book."

C. Jim Carr,
President, Blue Book Services, Inc.
Adjunct Instructor, Wheaton College, co-instructor,
Business Ethics and Management
Mayor of Wheaton, Illinois, 1993–2007

"The authors provide an excellent perspective on understanding ethics and politics. I am confident that this book will make a positive contribution to the field."

Kevin J. Jones, EdD
Assistant Professor of Management
Indiana University–Purdue University Columbus

"Ethical leadership is a challenging proposition for the most seasoned administrator. This book is a great tool for gaining confidence and learning strategies to address even the most difficult situations."

Craig Schilling, EdD
Advisor, Digital Schools LLC
Salinas, California

"This logical and significant link between ethics and school district politics provides a much-needed pragmatic model for emerging school leaders. The authors provide a reality-check on school organizational decision-making which is purposeful and reflective. They do not gloss over the difficult leadership factors which may make or break a school leader."

L. Arthur Safer, PhD
Professor, Department of Leadership, Concordia University Chicago
Professor Emeritus, Loyola University Chicago

"As a practicing superintendent, I realize that understanding the increasing role of politics in education is of utmost importance. This book gives school leaders real-world insight into how to balance ethics and politics in today's society."

Dr. Kevin J. O'Mara
Superintendent, Argo Community High School
President, Illinois High School District Organization

"Drs. Brierton, Graham, Tomal, and Wilhite team up to define ethics and provide specific examples that lead to a deeper understanding of challenges faced by today's educational leaders. Through concise explanations, case studies and discussion questions, leaders (veteran, novice) are provided invaluable insight to assist navigation of daily trials and tribulations."

Kimberly Strike, EdD
Associate Professor, Department of Leadership
Concordia University Chicago

"The authors provide an excellent perspective on the complex role of ethics and politics in education. I'm confident that this book will be of great value for all educators."

Melissa Dudic
Chair, Mathematics Department
Glenbard West High School, Illinois

"The authors provide a comprehensive and cogent consideration of school leaders navigating the turbulent political waters of administration. The book includes timely case studies to promote honing one's ethical thinking and perspectives. Well done!"

Kathryn G. Hollywood, PhD
President & CEO Cordis Educational Services
Prescott, Arizona

"The ability to ethically navigate the complexities of school politics is critical for educators and administrators alike. Brierton, Graham, Tomal, and Wilhite offer a poignant read with multiple perspectives to consider. This book is a practical and reliable resource."

Jean Papagiannis
Principal, Kilmer Elementary School
Chicago, Illinois

"When I teach my doctoral level class on the superintendency, I tell my students that most superintendents who get fired are not let go because they didn't understand curriculum, instruction, personnel, finance, facilities and the like. Instead, most unsuccessful superintendents failed because they could not grasp the intricacies and complexities of politics and ethics within the superintendent position. The authors of this new book do an effective job discussing politics and ethics, and do so from an experienced 'in the trenches' approach that cannot be matched. A highly worthwhile read for all administrators."

Dr. Joseph M. Porto
Former Superintendent
Avoca School District 37, Wilmette, Illinois

"Written by a group of experienced educational leaders, the book offers a valuable overview of theories and best practices to enable school administrators face political challenges and resolve ethical dilemmas with confidence and knowledge. Inclusion of case studies fosters careful consideration of real-life issues that are central to the work of educational leaders."

Elena Lyutykh, EdD
Assistant Professor of Research
Concordia University Chicago

"The authors provide an excellent perspective on understanding ethics and politics. I'm confident that this book will provide a positive contribution to the field."

Dr. Susan Sosoo
Assistant Principal, Administration/Organization
New York City Department of Education

"Even though a school administrator may have extensive content knowledge and leadership skills, these are not enough to provide quality leadership. Without a solid ethical and moral foundation, a leader is not respected, admired and committed to doing the right thing at the right time in the right place. The authors have integrated valuable information, depth of knowledge, concepts for reflection and analysis and challenges for intellectual growth. Understanding and implementing the principles in this book will enhance the quality of your leadership."

Ron Warwick, EdD
Professor, Department of Leadership
Concordia University Chicago

"In this well-written book, the authors demystify the critical (and hard) work of leadership in education by identifying the specific values and habits of proven leaders. The book challenges all education professionals to 'up their game' by more effectively applying character and competency to create greater value in this critically important investment of educating our future adult citizens and employees. This book is a 'must-read' for current education leaders at all levels and aspiring future leaders, as well as elected school board members!"

Richard Sibbernsen,
Retired Executive Vice President
AT&T Corporation

"This is an excellent reference for those who place a high value on an ethical approach to the political aspects of school leadership. These authors have adeptly shared their vast experience and expertise on this critical and current topic."

Alan E. Meyer, PhD
Executive Vice President
Concordia University Chicago

"It's more urgent now than ever before for educational leaders to effectively handle school politics in an ethical manner. The authors have applied their vast experience to develop this comprehensive work and I recommend this book—well done!"

Julie Davis, EdD
OAESA, Executive Director
Columbus, Ohio

"It has been said that effective school and district leaders must know the difference between right and wrong—and have the guts to stand up for what is right. This book provides comprehensive foundational principles for knowing, understanding, and taking appropriate actions when operating schools and school districts. It is a must-read for anyone considering a leadership career in public education."

George Zimmer, EdD
Associate Professor
Concordia University Chicago

"The authors demonstrate their comprehensive knowledge and experience in ethics, leadership, conflict resolution, negotiating, and much, much more. A dynamic tool for all educators."

Dr. Anthony J. Salerno
North Riverside, Illinois

"In an era of unprecedented pressure on school administrators and teachers, this much-needed book serves as an excellent resource to effectively handle the challenges of school politics in an ethical manner. The authors have applied their vast experience to develop this comprehensive work to help administrators thrive in their leadership roles and serve as ethical role models for the entire school community."

Peter Renn, EdD
Director, Center for Global Outreach
Concordia University Chicago

"Education is a precious social value but it is also highly problematic in contemporary culture. School leadership should therefore combine ethics and politics as this book comprehensively argues. I highly recommend his book."

Henk ten Have, MD, PhD
Director, Center for Healthcare Ethics
Duquesne University, Pittsburgh, Pennsylvania

"Recognizing the challenges that come with navigating politics and applying ethical principles in the school setting, the authors provide a comprehensive as well as practical text for school leaders. Clearly, they have a thorough understanding of both the obligation and commitment necessary to be successful in dealing with school politics."

Carolyn Theard-Griggs, EdD
Associate Professor of Curriculum, Language, and Literacy
Concordia University Chicago

"This book is not only a valuable resource for all educators on ethics and politics. I'm confident that this book will provide a positive resource. I highly recommend this book."

Beverly Pollard
Claims Operations Manager
Chubb & Son, a division of Federal Insurance Company, Arizona

"These authors know school leadership and ethics. Their extensive experience is evident in this book's approach to ethics and politics of schools. This is a valuable resource for all educators and school leaders."

Lorinda Sankey, PhD
Associate Dean, College of Education
Concordia University Chicago

"In an atmosphere of high stakes testing and accountability, the pressure on school leaders continues to increase. These pressures cause some to make decisions that are not based on the perspective of what is best for students. This book provides an effective guide for how to navigate the political waters of leadership while staying true to yourself, to your ethics, and to your belief systems."

Eric Hamilton
Assistant Principal, Curriculum and Instruction
Lake Zurich High School, Illinois

"From the perspective of my Lutheran education tradition, *Ethics and Politics in School Leadership: Finding Common Ground* is a catechism of ethical leadership principles for every school administrator. It raises the questions and provides concise answers to be explored and refined for specific classroom, administrative and leadership circumstances. Although its focus is on school leadership, it is an appropriate read for leadership in all walks of American life as all leadership interacts with culture, politics, business and education."

Craig Lusthoff, JD
Associate Dean, College of Business
Concordia University Chicago

"The ability to survive school politics is essential for effective leadership. This book is insightful and a valuable resource for all educators—I highly recommend this book!"

Julie Bryniczka,
Math Division Head,

Harry D. Jacobs High School, Illinois

"Leaders are often confronted with difficult choices. The text serves as a thoughtful reference for school leaders seeking to prioritize ethical decision-making while navigating the precarious realms of policy and politics. The text's checklists, frameworks and case studies provide structure to complex considerations of virtue, equity and justice—making this a soon-to-be beloved text for all leaders."

Dara Soljaga, PhD
Associate Professor of Curriculum, Language and Literacy
Concordia University Chicago

"This book is a must-read for anyone in or considering a position of leadership in education. The authors provide an outstanding perspective on ethics and politics in school organizations."

Kathleen S. Fritch, MS
Assistant Vice President, Partnerships & College Operations
Concordia University Chicago

"The authors have assembled an outstanding book about the relationship of ethics and politics in school leadership by incorporating experience, theory, and realistic case studies. The result is a scholarly book that will be a valuable resource for all educators, students, practitioners, and policymakers. I highly recommend this book!"

Lauren A. Wellen, EdD
Professor of Education
Concordia University Chicago

"This text is a valuable resource for school leaders who wish to employ ethical decision-making and better understand the political landscape of schools. The case studies are excellent."

Kristi Stricker, PhD
Professor of Education
Concordia University Chicago

"I highly recommend this book to all school administrators whose daily survival depends on the management of constant decision making in an ethical manner. As Aristotle said, 'Excellence is an art won by training and habituation: we do not act rightly because we have virtue or excellence, but we rather have these because we have acted rightly; "these virtues are formed in man by his doing the actions"; we are what we repeatedly do.' I strongly encourage the reading of this book."

Howard J. Bultinck, PhD
Associate Professor & Chair, Educational Leadership Department
Northeastern Illinois University, Chicago, Illinois

Contents

Foreword

It is an honor to write the foreword for this excellent and timely contribution to an ongoing debate about ethics. While *Ethics and Politics in School Leadership: Finding Common Ground* focuses on the particular arena named in its title, the discussion is part of a larger dialogue that must take place as we rethink what it means to ethically respond to the rapidly changing social and political context of education. In the pages that follow, distinguished professionals in school leadership have shared their experience and research to assist others by inviting them into the discussion. This volume in the Concordia University Leadership Series will serve educators well for many years to come.

In his great *Metaphysics*, Aristotle wrote, "It is the mark of an educated mind to be able to entertain a thought without accepting it." I suppose that is especially true in our time as competing ethical systems vie for dominance in the marketplace of ideas. In nearly any topic, what was once almost universally accepted as true and right is now but one of many competing claims to veracity and ethicality. At the same time, we can oversimplify the past and imagine it to be a time of uniformity and unity of mind and purpose. As any historian can tell us, that past actually exists only in the romantic imagination of those struggling with the complexities of their own day. So we are, in many ways, walking into the middle of a discussion that has gone on for a very long time and will continue into the future.

Aristotle's notion of entertaining ideas without accepting them is at the heart of the educational leader's vocation. There are multiple perspectives that rightly demand a hearing and consideration. At times the "marketplace of ideas" may seem to be much more of a "battleground" than a place of peaceful exchange. One of the finest leaders I have ever known was a lieutenant general in the U.S. Army, a veteran of 38 years as an infantry officer, who described leadership as "heading toward the sound of the gunfire." This I suggest is especially true in the area of educational leadership and ethics. Our schools and students need leadership that is unafraid to engage the most difficult and even divisive issues. There is a lot of listening to be done, many conversations to be had, and many difficult decisions to be reached. The true educational leaders, I believe, will be the ones who are the first into the fray and the last to leave.

It is not easy to lead in education. There are many constituencies that rightly demand a place at the table. Parents, school boards, faculty, administrators, staff, and others all have a vested interest in the decisions made by those whose vocation it is to lead. Add to this the demands of governmental oversight agencies, both federal and state, and the result may feel like a confused cacophony rather than a unified symphony. From this confusion, true leaders will emerge—leaders who listen, understand, and bring a clear vision and direction out of what might otherwise be chaos.

Ethics and Politics in School Leadership: Finding Common Ground is written to assist leaders in an increasingly diverse and complicated educational environment. At the center of it all is the "student"—not "students" as a nondescript mass of human beings but "student" as the individual and unique human being that sits in a classroom. Please read and engage with others about what you have read. Join the conversation!

The Reverend Daniel L. Gard, PhD
President
Concordia University Chicago

Acknowledgments

When I retired after thirty-seven years in public education, with ten of those years as a high school principal, I began to reflect on the political nature of these past positions. During my years as an adjunct professor of educational leadership, I often listened to my students' concerns about politics in their own schools. As aspiring leaders, they clearly were worried about how they might learn to navigate and survive the politics of school leadership. Their concerns prompted me to consider a leadership book on the subject of ethics and politics in schools.

Not long after joining the full-time faculty of the Department of Educational Leadership at Concordia University Chicago, I proposed the idea of such a book to my colleagues. They too agreed that there was a strong need, especially amidst the changes in public education today, for a text that could provide some experiential insight into issues of ethics and politics in schools. We all shared a common concern that school leaders, especially new leaders, might be inadequately prepared for the political aspects of the task at hand. And so this book was born.

When my colleagues and I met to discuss this project, I quickly realized how fortunate I was to be in the company of so much expertise and experience in school leadership. Gratitude is first extended to Dr. Robert Wilhite, Professor and Chair of the Department of Leadership at Concordia University Chicago, who not only graciously welcomed me to the department, but also enthusiastically supported the idea for this book. His leadership continues to serve as an example for me and for my colleagues.

A special acknowledgment is given to Dr. Daniel Tomal, Distinguished Professor of Leadership at Concordia, who not only created the *Concordia University Chicago Leadership Series*, but whose experience and expertise in the writing of this book has been invaluable to me. I am a much better writer because of Dan.

Acknowledgment is also given to Dr. Brenda F. Graham, who gave me my first opportunity to teach the Ethics course at Concordia University Chicago. Doing so formed the genesis of my own reflection on the importance of servant leadership and ethical leadership practice. Brenda's knowledge, experience, and commitment to instilling in our students the need for ethical leadership practice has greatly influenced and shaped my own teaching of this very important topic. As a junior member of the faculty, I am profoundly grateful for the opportunity to collaborate with my colleagues on this important book.

It is important to recognize Dr. Margaret Trybus, Associate Dean of the College of Graduate and Innovative Programs at Concordia University Chicago, who, many years ago, made a leap of faith and gave me my first opportunity to teach for Concordia University Chicago, as an adjunct faculty member. I am also grateful to Dr. Thomas Jandris, Dean of the College of Graduate and Innovative Programs, who welcomed me to Concordia University Chicago as a full-time faculty member and continues to encourage me in my work.

A sincere thanks is extended to Dr. Jennifer Placek, Associate Professor and Director of Internships and Partnerships. In this my first year as full-time faculty, Dr. Placek has served as my mentor and advisor, and I am grateful for her guidance and good counsel. I need also to recognize Dr. Ronald Warwick, Professor of Leadership at Concordia University Chicago, who taught me that patience, a sense of urgency, and a bias for action are necessary traits for transformational school leaders.

I want to recognize Dr. Susan Hirsch, Professor Emeritus of History at Loyola University Chicago, who was singularly responsible for my surviving the PhD dissertation process and whose kindness continues to remind me that empathy is an important trait for both teachers and leaders. It is also important to acknowledge Rowman & Littlefield Publishers for allowing me to coauthor and publish this book.

During my time in the U.S. Army Reserve, I was fortunate to serve with some exceptional leaders whose knowledge, experience, and instruction have profoundly shaped my own leadership philosophy. I am grateful for their leadership example as well as for their service to our country. They are the embodiment of servant leadership.

A very special recognition is given to my parents who did not often speak of leadership but lived it every day. They taught me to always lead from the front and that those who are courageous and care about people make the very best leaders.

This is my first book so special thanks must be given to my wife, Mary Beth, and my children, Peter, Genna, Henry, and Mike for their love, support, and humor throughout this project. They kept reminding me of what

P.G. Woodhouse said, "that the awful part of the writing game is that you can never be sure the stuff is any good." I trust my stuff is good.

Finally, acknowledgment is given to all those across the broad spectrum of education, history, business, and government who chose leadership as their life's work. They offer a wealth of knowledge and example for all to learn and emulate. Isaac Newton once remarked, "If I have seen further, it is because I have stood on the shoulders of giants." I am forever grateful to the giants in my life, and may all aspiring leaders ultimately find their own.

Jeffrey T. Brierton

The authors of this book acknowledge the hard work and dedication of all educators around the world who endeavor to prepare leaders of the future. We dedicate this book to them. Thanks to our families and colleagues for supporting us throughout our careers.

Introduction

School leaders at the district, building, and departmental levels are the primary agents of school improvement and change. We believe that there is a critical need to assist school leaders at all levels to influence school culture and to ethically navigate the politics of their school and district. Programs in higher education provide scant background and coursework in managing the ethics and politics of the school district. Without this support, school leaders, especially new and aspiring leaders, will be unable to achieve meaningful and sustainable change and improvement in our schools.

It is extremely important for today's school leaders to recognize and understand what occurs at the "intersection" of practice, ethics, and politics. Today's school leaders frequently must reconcile the dilemma of knowing what "needs to be done" (practice), knowing what "should be done" (ethics), and the need to build consensus for "getting it done" (politics). It is also important for the school leader to understand how to build an ethical school culture through the establishment of core values, open communication, and a culture of mutual respect.

School leaders are also being asked to lead far beyond the expectations of a decade ago. Those expectations continue to rise in the face of competition for increasingly limited resources. Much like the business community, school leaders are also expected to produce high-quality products (students) in a world-class organizational context that reflects ethical practice as well as the politics of the possible.

In the current climate of increased public scrutiny and high-stakes accountability, school leaders must lead teachers, staff, parents, and school boards to greater success for all students. Many of the old paradigms must be discarded as leaders and stakeholders discover that the "status quo" will no longer work if their schools and their graduates are to compete in a global marketplace.

While this book is primarily directed toward public schools, the strategies in this book can be effective for independent, private pre-K through 12 schools, and charter schools. The principles and strategies are practical and useful for any school educator or graduate student preparing to lead school improvement efforts and professional learning and growth.

Chapter 1 offers a brief overview of the ethical theories and practices that influence educational leadership. Discussions center around the moral obligations needed to resolve the multitude of ethical, cultural, social, and political dilemmas leaders face in their schools and districts. Special emphasis is placed on topics related to the personal integrity and morality of leaders, how leaders ethically influence followers, and the current challenges facing ethical leaders. A case study and exercises are provided at the end of the chapter.

Chapter 2 presents an overview of how public schools are designing district-specific policies to respond to demographic, political, legal, and moral changes in society. A discussion on the historical foundation of public schools is presented to assist in gaining an understanding of how local, state, and federal laws and mandates influence school practice. Special emphasis is placed on the dimensions of diversity and how school districts are developing and implementing goals and strategies to meet the needs of all students. A case study and exercises are provided at the end of the chapter.

Chapter 3 examines the role of school boards in the public and private school settings. Examples are presented to show that school boards are one of the closest democratically elected entities to the communities they serve. School boards provide a wide array of services and assistance to the community. Citizens gain access to school district services and initiatives through board politics and practices. Yet, what becomes evident in communities across America is the impact that politics plays on the governance and ethical framework of local school districts. A case study and exercises are provided at the end of the chapter.

Chapter 4 illustrates the relational politics between employee groups including teachers, noncertified support staff, and the building leadership team. This is a very useful chapter for building-level leaders. Using practical tips and advice, it emphasizes the need for the leader to manage or even eliminate politics within those groups in order to optimize work in schools. Case studies and exercises are provided at the end of the chapter.

Chapter 5 discusses the all-important relationship between unions and building-level leaders. The discussion includes roles, characteristics, and key attributes of leaders in both groups, the grievance process, and how state and federal reforms have impacted the politics of the union-administration relationship. Special emphasis is given to strategies for optimizing the relationship, sharing leadership, and avoiding the corrosive conflict that historically has characterized the union-administration relational dynamic. Exercises and a case study are included.

Chapter 6 covers the topic of negotiating and communicating with people. This is a practical chapter that starts with an overview of the negotiation process and steps in collective bargaining. The chapter also includes common tactics and counter tactics in negotiations and ends with several communications strategies that can help to build effective interpersonal communications between parties. Like the other chapters, a comprehensive case study is provided with exercises and discussion questions.

In closing, chapter 7 provides eight comprehensive case studies to challenge the reader in applying knowledge and skills to ethics and politics. They consist of topics in areas such as human resources, district, board, and community relationships, unions, and finance. The cases include multiple exercises and discussion questions for the reader to provide in-depth analysis and responses and are ideal for individual, class, and group activities.

FEATURES OF THE BOOK

This book provides an insightful reading for graduate students and practicing educators. It is unique in providing many engaging examples that can be applied to multiple settings and situations. One feature of the book is the correlation of each chapter's objectives with professional organizational standards such as the *Interstate Teacher Assessment and Support Consortium* (InTASC), the *Interstate School Leaders Licensure Consortium* (ISLLC), the *Educational Leadership Constituent Council* (ELCC), the *Teacher Leader Model Standards*, and the *Learning Forward Standards*.

Another valuable feature of the book is the incorporation of multiple ethical leadership strategies, teacher evaluation and instructional improvement processes, data and research, school improvement models, resources, and union-management relationships. The information is presented in a clear-cut and practical manner. The topics in this book are useful for any school educator who desires to learn principles and strategies for initiating and evaluating school improvement, improving student performance, and building positive board of education, district, and community partnerships.

Other features of this book include:

- the value of ethical and moral leadership in schools,
- practical examples of ethical and political situations and how to resolve them,
- illustrations of ongoing political models and strategies,
- a comprehensive description of resources needed for ethical leadership,

- examples of resolving political conflicts,
- a review of national, state, and local laws impacting diversity,
- a rationale for the shift away from traditional union-management models,
- strategies for effective negotiating and communicating among parties,
- strategies in building a district, school, and community culture for success.

ORGANIZATION OF THE BOOK

The organization of this book is such that educators can understand principles, models, and strategies for ethically leading district and school initiatives. Each chapter builds upon the other. However, each chapter is also distinct in itself, because it illustrates a specific topic as part of the development of the ethical culture of leadership. Also, each chapter includes basic theories and examples of applying these theories, case studies, and exercises for discussion. Lastly, the concluding chapter can be used as a capstone to the book for the readers to test their abilities through a series of case studies on ethics and politics.

Chapter 1

Doing the Right Thing

Ethics and School Leadership

OBJECTIVES

At the conclusion of the chapter you will be able to:

1. Recognize the need for and the role of ethics in educational leadership (ELCC 5; InTASC 9, 10; ISLLC 5; TLEC 2, 9).
2. Learn some useful approaches to ethical thinking (ELCC 5; InTASC 9; ISLLC 5; TLEC 9).
3. Analyze and reflect upon leadership approaches to ethical dilemmas (ELCC 5; InTASC 9, 10; ISLLC 5; TLEC 9).
4. Consider the ethical implications of school and district policies in planning and decision-making (ELCC 1; InTASC 9; ISLLC 1; TLEC 5, 7, 9).
5. Develop an ethical approach to educational leadership in a pluralistic and conflicting society, based upon objective, rational grounds (ELCC 5; InTASC 7, 9; ISLLC 5; TLEC 9).
6. Create a school culture and programs that focus resources to support all students' learning and development (ELCC 2; InTASC 1, 2, 3, 5, 6, 7, 9, 10; ISLLC 2; TLEC 1, 2, 4, 5 6, 9).

LEADERSHIP AND ETHICAL INQUIRY

School leaders are faced with a plethora of decisions on a daily basis. Developing, implementing, and evaluating school programs play a large part in the decision-making role of all school leaders. In addition, leaders are responsible for the management and operations of other school functions, including administrating school and community politics, responding to state and federal

1

policies and mandates, supervising teachers and staff, responding to student needs, directing budgetary and fiscal requirements, and controlling public relations. Each leadership decision may influence either people or the entire school environment in some way.

Reflective school leaders thoughtfully consider the consequences of their decisions. Ethics must become the organizational priority in making decisions. This requires that school leaders examine their own character and have inward virtues that direct their behaviors.

The ethical influences of educators and students who work and learn in schools were developed and established before they became members of the organization. People often define themselves collectively and identify their social identity mutually. They also share the same set of norms, beliefs, attitudes, values, and manners. It is reasonable to say that the group behaviors are significantly impacted by communal standards and principles.

In these school settings, stakeholders learn about appropriate behavior through observing the actions of the leader. They are also influenced by the way leaders take *responsibility* for results. Most importantly, behavior is fostered by how the leader connects and forms *relationships* with and among school participants. Effective school leaders understand that their *performance* can influence and impact positive social behaviors and school climates. The relationship is shown in figure 1.1.

Followers seek leaders who take *responsibility* for results by establishing high standards. The leaders are viewed as being experts in school

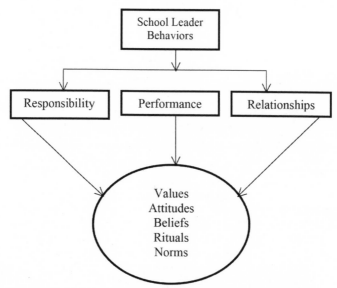

Figure 1.1   Leader behaviors and the communal standards they impact.

management and supervision, and are expected to address the needs and obligations of their job with knowledge and efficiency. Additionally, stakeholders expect leaders to be skillful decision makers and problem solvers. These leaders model responsibility for individual actions that is supported by transparency and anchored by a high personal value system.

The *performance* exemplified by moral leadership must model ethical behavior. Because the school climate is directly related to the leadership and management style of the leader, followers will directly or indirectly center their behaviors on the values, characters, skills, and priorities of the school leader. Leaders encourage dialogue and freedom of expression within the organization. They create a common sense of commitment and ownership among school stakeholders by inspiring engagement and collegiality.

Supportive, ethical leaders direct their *associations* toward meeting the diverse needs of followers. The interactions allow the stakeholders to have a voice in decision-making. Relationships with followers are measured by trust, fairness, courtesy, and care. Truly effective leaders also take time to listen to and meet the needs and concerns of followers.

Leadership must also apply virtue, which is moral character, to situations. How leaders behave is determined less by the policies, standards, and mandates than by their virtues. In essence, effective school leadership is built upon virtue, and virtue leads to trust. Ethical school leaders must exhibit moral excellence and have positive character traits and virtues that influence the formation of positive school cultures.

The virtue trait must be developed through deliberate and habitual practice. Ethical leaders are virtuous when they are committed to doing the right thing. Virtues shape the way ethical leaders behave. That is, virtues are habits of mind, heart, and behavior. Virtue may operate independently of a situation. Table 1.1 describes a list of virtues that ethical leaders must possess.

Integrity refers to the conduct of a leader who stands on high moral principles. The leader stands up for what is believed to be right and is ethically consistent in all action. He or she adheres to moral values and standards and works from a platform of honesty. Integrity must be the principal guiding force for all actions.

Table 1.1 Virtues associated with ethical leadership

Virtues	Descriptions
Integrity	Has high moral values and principles
Fairness	Able to make impartial judgments
Temperance	Exhibits self-control
Moral courage	Holds fast to values
Responsive listening	Engages in active listening

Fairness is exhibited when ethical leaders strive to seek justice for all stakeholders and make sure the needs of all are met. The leaders are fair in executing policies consistently. Effective school leaders strive to ensure that everyone in the school receives equal opportunity to be recognized, to learn, and to have impartial treatment. Fairness assures that everyone's voice is recognized and appreciated.

Temperance means demonstrating self-control, a trait which enables the leader to regulate and govern personal actions. Temperate leaders empower themselves to regulate every area of their lives. They have power to resist temptation and self-gratification. This trait also allows the leader to be self-sacrificing and responsive to the needs of stakeholders.

Moral courage is exemplified when leaders hold fast to their core values in times of uncertainty and unrest. Leaders who exemplify moral courage are reasonable when working with disagreeable and difficult personalities. Moral courage enables leaders to work effectively with those who oppose and disagree with ethical leadership on an ongoing basis. This action inspires moral commitment and assists in building honest school communities.

Responsive listening is a true sign that the leader is emotionally connecting with school participants. Responsive listening causes school stakeholders to feel safe and comfortable with the leader and each other. This builds trust and also encourages positive relational dynamics.

Knowledge of the virtues that guide leadership is essential for successful and ethical decision-making in schools. Moral sensibility is promoted when the leader is guided by virtuous conduct. The positive influence of this type of leader will stimulate confidence and trust among stakeholders.

Ethical school cultures are influenced by ethical leadership behaviors. By understanding this relationship, aspiring leaders can gain an enhanced insight into the role of ethical school leadership. These school leaders will quickly discover that many facets of their work will involve consideration of ethical issues. They will also quickly learn that ethical leaders are charged with positively inspiring and mentoring others to support and frame principled and moral school behaviors.

So, what exactly is ethics? The word ethics is derived from the Greek word ethos. The term originated from both Latin and Greek derivatives that produce the terms "ethical" and "character." Character is a form of moral behavior and can be originated and shaped by religious influence, the culture in which one lives, and the social norms of society. Accordingly, ethics in the context of school leadership is defined as rules of conduct or character that govern human behavior in schools.

Ethics reflect beliefs about what is right, what is wrong, what is just, what is unjust, what is good, and what is bad in terms of moral and social conduct. It is also measured by written and unwritten standards and principles.

Therefore, ethical leadership is the ability to model decision-making and behaviors that influence followers to behave ethically. This behavior is not stagnant and is based upon how situations are perceived, analyzed, and acted upon.

Effective school leaders willingly assume the obligation of ethical leadership when they make decisions in schools. They make decisions based on the legal, moral, and ethical implications of political options and policy requirements. Ethical decision-making is applied to changing situations on a daily basis and is defined in different ways. The following descriptions will assist in gaining essential knowledge on how different ethical principles are defined and viewed.

Value-based ethics refers to the organizational dynamic where strong morals and values drive accomplishment and bring clarity to what is important. It is positive and emphasizes group standards and norms. In essence, the values reflect the result of a collaborative process involving leadership and all stakeholders. Moreover, the school organization collectively acts in consistent ways to build a healthy school culture.

Cultural relativism reflects the belief that the interests of individuals and groups are relative, and that individual and group behaviors can be determined by cultures and backgrounds. Cultural relativists interpret morality as the product of culture and believe that people do not have any right to judge the ethics of another culture, except on its own terms. They also believe that there are no objective values. Cultural relativism must be a guiding factor for decision-making in diverse and changing school environments.

The principle of *rule-based ethics* is based upon the premise that all are treated fair and equitably if a prescribed set of rules based upon honesty, justice, and fairness is adhered to by all. Ethical behavior involves following rules of peer group, culture, family, and other organizations. The rules set guidelines that all are expected to follow. Articulating and communicating the rules is a prerequisite for optimal adherence.

Situational ethics considers the context of situations, not fixed laws, in decision-making. That is, what is right depends on the particular circumstance. Situational ethics will often be used to resolve the numerous dilemmas faced by today's school leaders. These leaders use the most appropriate approach to align decision-making and results.

The use of knowledge that is governed when a specific service is provided to the public is considered *professional ethics*. Professionals and those working in recognized professions provide services to the public. These services can be considered moral when judgments are made that are based upon knowledge, expertise, and experience. Expert professional knowledge is a critical component for school leaders as they strive for effectiveness in working with staff, students, parents, and other stakeholders in school settings.

Descriptive ethics are used to understand the motives that cause behaviors and seek to understand how the sense of wrong or right develops in individuals. Creating codes to regulate the conduct of members in an organization is an example of the use of descriptive ethics. Because beliefs are based on background and culture, psychologists use descriptive ethics to study moral reasoning.

Every aspect of the school's culture can be affected by the decision-making of school leaders. They provide direction and exercise influence in schools and districts. Positive leadership authority incorporates the principles of moral leadership. Effective school leaders create alignments between strong value systems and the practice of those values in the decision-making process. That is why it is important for the school leader to understand and be aware of his or her moral compass and core values.

To be moral means to have a deep sense of ethics and to be motivated by values that support the pursuit of justice and equity in all relations. Moral leadership necessitates the ability to think objectively, with an unbiased opinion, through moral issues. Thus, moral leadership involves ethical conduct on the part of leaders in inspiring ethical conduct in followers.

Moral leaders challenge themselves to be ethical. Their conduct and behavior validate their effort to meet that challenge. Their leadership influences others through ethical relationships marked by respect and empowerment. Therefore, the moral school leader demonstrates ethical conduct and behaviors that initiate, inspire, and motivate ethical performance by all within the school culture.

Effective school leaders drive success when they have extensive knowledge of the instructional and curricular needs of their organizations. An understanding of how to use research and data to drive decision-making is a necessary requisite of successful leadership. The ability to meet diverse student needs, form collaborative relationships with staff, and drive community partnerships is also an essential quality.

An example of a type of effective leader is the transformational leader. Transformational leadership empowers and inspires members by communicating a clear vision of the group's goals through inspiration and enthusiasm. The vision can create followers with energy, excitement, and commitment that stimulate and arouse passion for the work. The followers are then provided clear and ongoing direction and guidance that assist in making the vision a reality.

The initial concept of transformational leadership was introduced by James MacGregor Burns (1978), who aligned the concepts of motivation and values in determining leadership power. According to the idea of transformational leadership, an effective leader is a person who helps followers grow and develop into leaders by responding to individual followers' needs.

Transformational leadership in schools is accomplished when the school leader empowers school participants by:

- Articulating and inspiring a vision of what is to come.
- Encouraging and motivating followers.
- Working alongside the team to produce a positive outcome.

Transformational school leaders have a strong sense of moral purpose and create agendas dedicated to working purposefully and collaboratively with school stakeholders to create moral environments. There are, however, other leadership styles that work effectively in schools. They are servant, moral, and instructional leadership. Figure 1.2 describes some characteristics of ethical leadership.

Servant leadership is based upon a responsibility to moral principles and a commitment to give stakeholders what they need in order to be successful in their duties and obligations. Servant leaders guide by example, have integrity, and create positive school cultures that lead to high morale among teachers and other school staff. The relationships evolve as a result of principals who put the needs of others first. Significantly, servant leadership emphasizes the use of honesty and encouragement rather than control.

Moral leadership describes the type of leadership that is guided by school leaders who supervise and manage with personal integrity. Moral leadership is motivated by high ethical standards that are always exemplified by a deep

> - The leader influences by articulating vision and motivating by example.
>
> - The leader influences by ensuring that the followers' needs are of highest priority.
>
> - The leader influences by applying moral and ethical standards to duty.
>
> - The leader influences by focusing on instructional improvement.

Figure 1.2   Characteristics of ethical leaders.

sense of ethics and motivated by the pursuit of a higher purpose. The primary intention is to serve others with honesty and integrity. These leaders are empathetic and very skillful communicators.

Instructional leadership incorporates organizational management skill for instructional practices. The leader focuses on learning that is essential for both students and teachers, and addresses the cultural, linguistic, socioeconomic, and learning differences in the school. Effectiveness is measured by improvement in instruction and in the quality of student learning.

These educational leaders serve the school and community by providing equal and ethical opportunities for students to learn. An "ethical school leader" shapes the ethical context of the school through moral influence. Service-oriented conduct that is based upon sensitivity to the needs of stakeholders and the school is exemplified in all actions.

Ethical school leaders model personal and professional ethics in how they manage themselves and how they work with others. They follow a prescribed set of standards and principles in carrying out their duties and responsibilities. The actions are sustained when the following principles are maintained. The leader:

- Ensures that the educational well-being of students is founded upon sound ethical and moral principles.
- Is accountable for personal actions and behaviors and committed to serve all school stakeholders with integrity and accountability.
- Exhibits honesty and integrity in fulfilling personal and professional duties.
- Knows and develops knowledge and skills that can be used to promote continuous school improvement.
- Understands the organizational change process and knows how to build a supportive school culture.

ETHICAL AND MORAL REASONING

Ethics are based upon logically constructed ideologies. Ethical behavior considers what is right or what should be done in the face of uncertainty or conflict. Ethical practices in schools and other organizations are clearly defined and widely accepted. Therefore, ethics are applied to standards or codes of behavior that individuals and groups are expected to follow.

These ethical actions are facilitated by using moral principles to inform decision-making. The use of *moral principles* is the process in which individuals and groups determine right and wrong conduct. By using moral principles, school leaders make attempts to assess the decision-making outcome they need in order to come to logical conclusions. Implicitly, principals and school leaders use moral reasoning daily as a tool in decision-making.

To apply moral principles to situations, we must first be able to define whether or not the action was right, wrong, or that the action was neutral. For example, we might say that a gunman who comes into a school and commits mass murder is an evil person, or that the destruction of a school by a tornado is a bad thing. We may even say that a police officer who kills a resistant citizen is committing a rightful act. The focus in each situation would be on the morality of the act.

The process breaks ethical behavior down into four psychological components which is based upon the work of Rest, Narvaez, Bebeau, and Thoma (1999). The psychologists concluded that ethical action is the product of the following psychological subprocesses: *moral sensitivity* (recognition), *moral reasoning* (judgment), *moral motivation*, and *moral character*. Table 1.2 shows the progression of leadership components and actions.

Moral sensitivity occurs when the school leader recognizes the existence of an ethical issue or problem. That knowledge assists in understanding and determining the effect the action will have on others. With that knowledge, the school leader will be able to envision various courses of action to take and determine the consequences of each action. Moral sensitivity increases leadership consideration and enhances the decision process.

Moral reasoning is the process of deciding between what is right and what is wrong in personal situations by utilizing reasoning and sound judgment. In order to come to logical conclusions, leaders must first have knowledge of what the action intended to accomplish. They will also need to know how the consequences of the act will affect others. In a true sense, moral reasoning is based upon individual points of views regarding what is right and what is wrong in any given situation.

Moral motivation allows the leader to uphold the virtues of integrity and moral courage. The leader's style of behavior must be intentionally moral. These virtues are essential when the actions of others are in conflict with the norms, values, and culture of the school. Establishing and implementing clear standards and policies will alleviate most unconstructive behaviors among followers.

Table 1.2   Progression of leadership moral components and actions

Steps	Moral Components	Ethical Action
One	Moral Sensitivity	Identifies an ethical dilemma
Two	Moral Reasoning	Makes an ethical judgment
Three	Moral Motivation	Formulates an ethical intention
Four	Moral Character	Generates ethical character

Source: Rest, Narvaez, Bebeau, and Thoma, 1999

Moral character enables leaders to overcome obstacles and discouragements that may result from taking principled stances. It is based upon upright and honorable behavior and the belief that all actions of a person with moral character are performed with duty in mind.

The concept of moral reasoning is based upon the American psychologist Lawrence Kohlberg's theory of moral development (1973). Kohlberg developed a theory that was derived from empirical evidence. The evidence revealed that individuals pass through moral stages of development. The stages start in early childhood and progress to adulthood. Kohlberg's theory is often used to explain moral thinking as applied to decision-making.

At the lowest level of moral development, people make choices that will assist them in avoiding punishment and gaining rewards. This is called *preconventional* thinking, and the focus is upon consequences. In the *conventional* level of moral development, individuals begin to respect and value the concerns of others and begin to focus on the rules and laws that govern their behavior. Individuals reach the advanced stage of moral development when choices are made based upon social concerns related to group and team outcome. This stage is called *postconventional* morality. The levels of moral development and their stages are summarized in Table 1.3.

Preconventional Level of Moral Development (Level 1) centers on the concepts of obedience and punishment.

- Stage one decision-making choices involve following rules in order to avoid punishment.
- Stage two decision-making choices are evident when individuals make decisions according to selfish motives and based on receiving rewards.

Conventional Level of Moral Development (Level 2) focuses on the premise that individuals follow the normal or established behaviors of society.

Table 1.3   Kohlberg's levels of moral development

LEVEL ONE: PRECONVENTIONAL	
Stage One	Rules are followed in order to avoid punishment.
Stage Two	The moralities of actions are based upon selfish motives.
LEVEL TWO: CONVENTIONAL	
Stage Three	Behaviors are performed in certain ways in order to seek approval.
Stage Four	Adherence to laws, rules, and policies is in order to maintain social order.
LEVEL THREE: POSTCONVENTIONAL	
Stage Five	Decision-making choices are based upon perceived conformity to social justice and human dignity.
Stage Six	Individuals develop their own set of moral guidelines based upon what they perceive as justice.

Source: Lawrence Kohlberg, 1973

- Stage three decision-making occurs when individuals make decisions and behave in certain ways in order to seek approval or live up to the expectations of others.
- Stage four choices are evident when the individual decision-making agenda is oriented to adherence to laws, rules, and policies in order to maintain social order.

Postconventional Level of Moral Development (Level 3) concentrates on following the utilitarian principles of ethical behavior.

- Stage five decision-making choices are guided by an understanding of the importance of human dignity and social justice.
- Stage six decision-making choices are guided by individuals' development of their own set of moral guidelines based upon what they perceive as justice.

School leaders must make and defend sound decisions in school environments with stakeholders from diverse backgrounds with differing lifestyle norms and values. It is inevitable in these types of environments that critical tensions and competing values will exist. Effective leaders must balance the conflicts arising from the variable needs of the students, parents, teachers, and community with their roles as manager, instructional leader, and supervisor. This obligates them to demonstrate knowledge and skills needed to monitor and implement proactive decision-making strategies that encourage objective insight and positive results.

Ethical decision-making utilizes a systematic process to address ethical concerns. When making ethical decisions, school leaders must have systems in place to shape the process. Those structures will guide the process and enable the school leader to address ethical conflicts expeditiously. They will also address ethical questions and dilemmas on a level that will be mutually beneficial to all.

Strategies are incorporated to define methods and procedures. These include guidelines and written standards and policies to direct the decision-making process. With the strategies in place, inconsistency and contradictory actions involving school stakeholders can be reflectively identified and lessons can be learned for future decisions.

Many decisions school leaders make are routine. However, leaders face unpredictable dilemmas that require a strategic response. They occur when stakeholder values come into conflict with the norms and values of the school, or with other members of the school community. In those cases, an essential function of educational leadership is to make decisions that are in the best interest of the school and its stakeholders.

In order to facilitate the creation of positive solutions to ethical dilemmas in schools, principals must work collaboratively with school stakeholders to create a framework of ethical standards and requirements that will guide ethical decision-making. The planning team should be representative of individuals with diverse perspectives. Principled standards and ethical behavior criteria should be the benchmarks of the planning process.

Altruism, teamwork, empathy, and cooperation are the values that define the moral and ethical qualities needed in schools. These qualities translate into high expectations for students and adults. They should be discussed during job interviews, and they should also be aligned with all decision-making planning and processes.

Altruism is a value that incorporates the traits of consideration, thoughtfulness, generosity, and unselfishness in manner and conduct. This value should be reflected in all school interactions. These include activities and relationships that take place during the regular school day. Altruism should also occur as school-based community relationships are developed.

Teamwork allows for group partnerships that support and value individual contributions. Cooperation and mutual support are the frameworks of this value. Collegial and shared relationships are essential components of effective school cultures. The greatest resources any school leader can acquire are obtained through teaming.

Empathy begins with understanding viewpoints that hold opposing opinions. This trait is fundamental in creating atmospheres of trust and friendship. Leaders who are empathetic provide encouragement at all times. Empathy is essential for embracing diversity, building relationships, and acquiring tolerance.

Cooperation occurs when school leaders maintain a solid school climate that effectively engages all supporters. They should be mutually supportive of all stakeholders. Mutual consideration allows school members to exchange valuable information and knowledge. These relationships can make the difference between academic success and failure.

Understanding ethical theory is vital to arriving at solutions needed to make decisions regarding moral and ethical dilemmas. These ethical theories are divided into three broad types: *Consequentialist, Nonconsequentialist,* and *Virtue.* Individually, each gives emphasis to different aspects of an ethical dilemma.

Consequentialist theories are mainly concerned with the ethical consequences of particular actions. They are concerned with persons making ethical decisions that are based upon moral evaluation of acts, rules, and institutional guidelines. Consequentialists hold that the outcome of decision-making is based solely upon effect and ultimate consequence. Ethical theories or approaches that are placed in this category are the utilitarian theory and the common good theory.

- *Utilitarianism* maintains that the best action will be the one which provides the most good or does the least harm. On a global basis, the approach supports the idea that ethical actions within groups are the ones that produce the greatest good and do the least harm for all who are affected.
- The *Common Good Approach* contends that good societies should be guided by the will of the people. That general will would then produce what is best for the people as a whole. This approach to ethics emphasizes respect and compassion for others, especially those who are more vulnerable.

Nonconsequentialist theories judge the rightness or wrongness of an action based on properties fundamental to the act. The properties are seen as intrinsic. The act itself is not judged. Ethical theories or approaches that are placed in this category are the *deontology*, the *rights approach*, and the *fairness and justice approach*.

- Deontology holds that some choices cannot be justified by their effects. It also maintains that no matter how morally good the consequences, some choices are morally forbidden. The theory argues that individuals must follow morally ethical obligations.
- The Rights Approach claims that the best ethical approach is the one which protects the rights of individuals who are affected by the action. This theory focuses on respect for human dignity. Rights advocates argue that individuals should be able to claim certain privileges because of necessity.
- The Fairness and Justice Approach holds that all should be treated fairly and that equals should be treated equally, and unequals unequally. Giving each person the rights and liberties due him or her is a contention of this ethical theory.

The *virtue approach* does not de-emphasize rules and consequences and centers on the personality of the individual. This term is broad and is not divided into specialized types or approaches. This virtue approach to ethics focuses on individual characters or dispositions and is concerned with the whole person, not individual actions of the person. In this approach, character, and not action, is evaluated.

Ethical theories and *principles* are the foundations of ethical analysis because they are the viewpoints from which guidance can be obtained along the pathway to a decision. Each theory emphasizes a different approach to logical decision-making. Ethical theories are useful when they are directed toward a set of goals. These principles are rules of standards of behavior and do not change with new information or different stakeholder involvement.

Ethical principles also specify universal standards of right and wrong on which to propose judgments relative to ethical theories. They also establish criteria for judgments. Some of the principles used by decision makers in making informed decisions theories are *beneficence, least harm, respect for autonomy and justice.*

Beneficence is an ethical term that denotes moral excellence or goodness. The welfare of all school stakeholders is the focus of outcome. This principle guides the ethical leader to do what is good or best for all. The essential demand is that the result of the decision should achieve the greatest amount of good because people benefit from the most good.

Utilizing the principle of least harm requires choosing the lesser of two evils when making decisions. The principle is somewhat similar to the beneficence principle. However, it only works with cases where neither of the behaviors was positive. In those cases, the leader should choose the one that is less harmful.

Respect for autonomy maintains that protection be given to vulnerable populations that may be incapable of performing or understanding information. The individualized educational plans of these individuals should be periodically reevaluated and updated. Another term for this ethical principle is *respect for person.* Districts must provide a range of services to meet the individual needs of students who have trouble succeeding in school because of disabilities.

The ethical principle of justice suggests that decision-making should provide results that are fair. It argues that justice does not mean treating all individuals the same. The justice theory argues that decisions should be fair and aligned with the extenuating circumstances that justify actions. Ethical school leaders must be deliberate and reflective of the school's mission and values when making decisions related to diverse populations.

It is essential that ethical decision-making is supported by the application of a written ethics framework. The framework reflects the principles and theories discussed earlier in the chapter. Fundamentally, it must rely on the principle of justice (fairness and equity). Three necessary characteristics of a useful ethical framework are given below (Workgroup for Community Health and Development, 2013):

- *Internal consistency* dictates that principles must fit with each other and not contradict each other.
- *Proactivity* requires that ethical frameworks are explicitly written and discussed with school stakeholders.
- *Dynamism* assures that the decision-making framework is examined on a regular basis and readjusted when needed.

A framework for ethical decision-making in schools is presented in this section. It is aimed at improving ethical decision-making by presenting a comprehensive framework that clarifies the process of solving ethical dilemmas. The framework must also be adaptable enough to transcend the entire school. The seven-step framework that can be used to resolve school-based ethical dilemmas includes:

1. Identify and define the ethical dilemma.
   - Define the dilemma by discussing the facts and issues of the situation.
2. Identify the stakeholders involved and determine their relationship to each other.
   - Who was impacted by the dilemma?
   - If so, how were they affected?
3. Review relevant policies pertinent to the dilemma.
   - These should include the school mission, values, and policies related to the situation.
   - If needed, consult with informed sources (district personnel, legal counsel, law enforcement personnel, etc.).
4. Reflect upon the possible courses of action needed for resolution.
   - List several alternative decisions and the pros and cons of each.
5. Decide on the best action.
6. Act on your decision
7. Reflect on the outcome. What are the lessons learned?

CREATING A CULTURE OF ETHICAL PRACTICE

Ethical thinking involves the process used to consider the influence of actions on individuals or groups within schools. One of the primary responsibilities of ethical leadership is to facilitate the integration of ethical principles in every area of school activity. This leadership has the ability to influence behaviors and shape the interactions shared among members of the school culture. A benefit of this process is a resulting dynamic and positive school climate or environment that inspires the best in all.

School climate may be defined as the overall attitude and character of school life. The climate represents current conditions that exist in schools. School leaders begin the process of building ethical climates by first creating environments of trust. By providing timely feedback, challenging inequities, and supporting all stakeholders, ethical school leaders can create positive, ethical climates. These positive school climates produce effective and strong school cultures.

School culture develops as school leaders, staff, students, and community members interact with each other. Establishing a culture of ethical practice requires school leaders to establish a social context within the school where participants form self-regulating ethical behaviors as a matter of routine.

This requires that the school leader demonstrates values-based leadership habits and traits. Some of the principles of values-based leadership include:

- Self-reflection and awareness.
- The ability to see situations from multiple viewpoints.
- The ability to recognize personal strengths and weaknesses and strive for improvement.
- The need to value all individuals.

When school leaders maintain and support high ethical standards and values, they influence ethical behavior within the entire school culture. The teachers and staff become more engaged and committed, teacher motivation increases, the attitudes among teachers toward their jobs improve, and students develop higher motivation to achieve.

Other characteristics of schools with strong ethical cultures are:

- Stakeholders share mutual goals and beliefs that shape practices.
- High expectation for all students is modeled by teachers.
- Student-centered instruction occurs in all classrooms.
- Principals and teachers view themselves and their environment as being collaborative.
- High student achievement is the school's focus.
- Classrooms are arranged to foster collaboration and relationship building.

A simple system that defines, reinforces, and defends the desired organizational culture is necessary to building an ethical school culture. Elements inherent in building cultures are *values, attitudes and beliefs, norms, and rituals*. These are all formed from communications, relations, and exchanges in the school environment over time. The elements and leadership roles needed for creating ethical cultures are reviewed. A diagram of the organizational culture is presented in figure 1.3.

Values are core beliefs that function as explicit foundational commitments to students and the school community. Values must be articulated and reinforced during meetings and interactions with all stakeholders. These stakeholders may include faculty, students, staff, parents, and other community partners. Of course, school leaders must consistently reflect the values in their own behavior.

Values also represent beliefs and the notion of right and wrong. They articulate the school's priorities and are the foundation behind choices made by school leaders. Essentially, values express what is important in schools and direct the behavior of individuals. Values shape the fundamental beliefs of the school and become core in nature. Having a set of core values is essential to driving ethical behavior in schools.

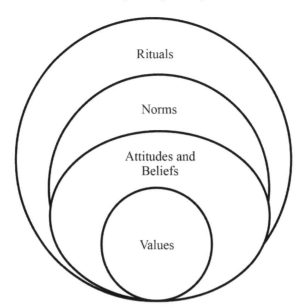

Rituals

Norms

Attitudes and
Beliefs

Values

Figure 1.3   Diagram of the organizational culture.

Core values should be reflected in the culture of the school and should drive all school practices. All school decisions on policy, practice, and programs should be aligned with the school's core values. The core values should also assist in the formation of good personal and social skills. All members of the school are obligated to adhere to the core values. This includes the administrators, teachers, and students.

Attitudes and Beliefs shape and influence every aspect of how a school functions. Teachers' perceptions of children and their families are strongly affected by personal beliefs and expectations. Just as the perceptions, attitudes, beliefs, and values of teachers impact instruction, student beliefs and attitudes influence classroom behavior and student conduct. Children come to school with diversities of ethnicities, cultures, languages, and habits. Each is linked with a distinct background and cultural setting, and students must all believe that they are respected and have value and worth.

Sociolinguistic researchers have shown that cultures of different sociocultural classes are remarkably different. Conflict in schools may occur when these children are taught by members of the teaching staff who are not aware of their lifestyles and have difficulty relating to them.

Ethical school leaders must find ways to institutionalize culturally responsive environments. They must also work with internal and external stakeholders in the design of educational services that will assist the staff in adapting to, and better serving, diverse populations. Character and diversity training, or some other form of moral training, should be an ongoing function of the curriculum.

Norms are defined as informal rules that govern behavior and influence the school culture. They are standards that are formalized and enforced by the school's social system. The norms are shared, integrated into the belief system, and sanctioned by the group. In ethical school environments, they should serve as prescriptions for moral behavior, provide a sense of safety and belonging, and add meaning and order to the school climate.

Over time, norms within the school organization may often be unconsciously adhered to. Conformity is taken for granted by group members. However, individuals who are new to the school or those who are from different ethnic or religious backgrounds may have conflicting behaviors that derive from contrasting cultural or religious conditions. As a result, they usually have no course of action except to conform to the norm, or be alienated. The skilled leader recognizes this situation and strives to make everyone feel welcome and accepted.

Rituals are formal and informal processes, traditions, and customs that are consistently practiced within the school culture often on a daily basis. Children standing and walking in line for recess is an example of a ritual. The salute to the flag, defining class rank, graduation exercises, and recognizing the student or teacher of the month are also rituals. It is in these ordinary, everyday activities that school participants bond and understand each other, regardless of class, ethnicity, or academic rank. Rituals also reinforce behaviors and indicate school values.

Ethical school leaders understand that education is not only about imparting knowledge. They recognize their roles as ethical leaders and managers. This obligates them to use the rituals and traditions of the school's culture to promote positive school climates. For example, they can promote and practice positive skills of communication, cooperation, conflict resolution, and empathy by making these a part of the fabric of staff training.

It is essential that all children are treated with dignity and respect. Cultural and moral training and practices will assist them in understanding the behaviors and needs of their students. They can then model and infuse the knowledge and skills they learn in their classrooms.

THE ORGANIZATIONAL ROLE OF ETHICS
IN INFLUENCING SOCIAL CHANGE

The terms "school culture" and "school climate" can have overlapping meanings. School culture represents the values, attitudes and beliefs, norms, and rituals that are shared by members of a school. School climate refers to the quality of the character and patterns of behaviors that are produced by the school culture and is grounded by the patterns of school relationships. Leadership performance, teacher relationships and skills, norms, goals, values, interpersonal relationships, and organizational structure define the school climate.

A supportive school climate contributes to positive student learning and school success. It is one where all school members are engaged and respect each other. The members work collaboratively to address school concerns and respond to social changes. This calls for transformational leadership where principals work with the school staff to assist in responding to those changes. The transformational leader helps build shared meaning among members of the school staff.

It can be argued that the 2001 No Child Left Behind (NCLB) federal statute raises the need for ethical school leadership to an entirely new level. The era of reform and change ushered in by this legislation requires that administrators gather and use academic data in an honest and ethical manner while also using strategic thinking and innovations to develop partnerships with a variety of constituencies. Recent changes in policies and mandates such as NCLB and numerous other new social trends have required school leaders to be responsible for molding the organization to implement best practices related to the social conditions that affect schooling.

Social change refers to any change over time in behavior patterns, cultural values, and norms of schools. Change may be in the form of political forces, economic pressures, emerging beliefs and values of society, and new technological innovations. All are certain to influence educational practices. Some of the issues of the twenty-first century that are influencing social change are discussed below.

Standards-based reform is a systemic approach designed to improve accountability systems and curriculum framework. Reform policies and mandates to schools are always shaped by historical, social, economic, and political changes over time. Numerous local, state, and federal policies and mandates require schools to focus on content, diversity issues, teacher quality, community engagement, classroom and teaching standards, academic content requirements, and assessment for learning outcomes.

Economic shifts are influencing spending across states and school districts. In many instances, states are providing less per-pupil funding for schools. Those cuts undermine education reform and hinder school districts' ability to deliver high-quality education. In addition, schools are using fewer resources to teach students in larger classrooms. To counter those mandates, school districts are undertaking innovative plans to improve teaching and learning.

Diversity issues are causing some concern in schools and districts. Children of diverse ethnicities, race, cultures, and socioeconomic classes are increasingly entering schools in America. These changes bring additional challenges to schools. Consequently, policies must be developed to assist teachers as they instruct an increasingly diverse population of students.

Technology and *global education* have created an increasingly connected world. They give students, educators, parents, and the community access to vast school and educational resources. In a space of a little over two decades, school life has been influenced through connections to the internet. Many schools will have to procure additional funding and revise or create policies to manage those changes.

School violence and *bullying* are key safety issues in schools. Violence in school takes many forms, and the frequency of this violence across America continues to be a rising safety concern for both schools and communities. School leaders are increasingly addressing ways to address these situations.

Effective school leaders recognize that the success of their schools is undeniably linked with broader ethical and social issues. They also understand that sustainable cultural efficiency is not possible without considering the effects and demands of larger social, political, and economic demands on how schools are managed and shaped. Notably, an understanding of the roles of values, attitudes and beliefs, norms, and rituals can assist the leaders in engaging outside school partnerships. Shaping school policy for effective results produces the following conditions in schools:

- Relationships become healthy and free of discrimination and harassment.
- Teachers and principals find solutions to problems through research, experience, and data investigation.
- Students are encouraged to be positive role models and leaders and speak up for issues such as bullying.
- All members of the school community are actively engaged in an ongoing dialogue.
- Individualism and teamwork become fundamental to the well-being of the school.
- Principles of equity and inclusion are embedded across the curriculum.
- Learning and instructional resources, teaching strategies, and assessment patterns reflect the diversity of all learners.
- Staff and students are inspired and given support to succeed.

ROLE OF THE ETHICAL LEADER AND STUDENT POLICIES

Schools are politically and socially complex organizations. As discussed previously, many schools serve diverse populations of students who come from different cultures and have different educational requirements. Students bring different lifestyle and value systems, each of which is associated with various degrees of child-rearing practices. Many teachers are from different ethnicities than the children they serve.

To meet the needs of all students in schools and to afford them equal enjoyment of fundamental rights, state, federal, and local mandates require procedures be in place that provide uniform treatment in every area of school life. To this end, schools and other organizations are required by law to have written policies on a number of areas for which they have responsibility. In other words, the rights, privileges, or responsibilities imposed on an identified segment of the school population must apply equally to all members of the school.

Policies are sets of rules, regulations, and procedures that establish the parameters that govern organizations. All organizations must have policies and procedures in place. A school's policies and procedures are adopted from laws passed by government agencies (federal, state, and local). These are in place to ensure the school is run effectively and that staff, pupils, and any other individuals involved with the school are protected from unreasonable restrictions.

While some policies are required by the federal government, districts and schools also develop their own policies and procedures. These are known as school-based policies. School-based policies are developed to ensure that system policies are implemented in a manner relevant to the school or in response to a specific school need. These policies and procedures are significant to staff, students, and parents and must be updated regularly.

School policies usually fall under two distinct categories: sets of decisions and actions, and sets of rules, regulations and decisions. An example of a "sets of decisions and actions" policy is a set of procedures that dictate the instructions to follow when a gunman enters the building. An example of a "regulations and decisions" policy is guidelines on how teachers instruct using certain curriculum materials that are related to standardized tests.

Effective leaders are also aware that an ethical culture requires a carefully planned and well-implemented code of conduct. The code must have clear policies and procedures aimed at guiding behaviors and influence decision-making. The organizational mission and values must be aligned with the standards of behavior. The needs of all levels of stakeholders in the school must be addressed in the code. The code of ethics should also be aligned with existing school policy and have a set of guidelines.

For the most part, school leaders must ensure that all members of the school community are well informed about the codes of conduct. The code should be comprehensive and provide policies to govern the conduct of students, teachers, and other school personnel. Professional development should be provided to personnel who have responsibilities in the areas impacted by the standards. The code should be monitored and reviewed at regular intervals.

Schools should also have handbooks for both certified and support staff. A handbook for substitute teachers is also an essential requirement. The policies should set expectations that significant stakeholders are held accountable for. They should be informative, clear, and succinct. These handbooks may be published in different languages depending on the population of the school and the community.

The school leader should also have plans in place for a committee to review and evaluate current policies to ensure that existing ones are still pertinent. Often, and depending upon changes in society or trends at the time, amendments or rewriting may be needed to keep policies up-to-date. The review committee should be made up of the school leader, school staff, students, and parents. It is essential that all current policies be available to individual stakeholders.

Lastly, a summary of the students' handbook must be provided to all students at a school assembly, or in homerooms, at the beginning of each school year. A copy should also be sent or mailed to all parents or guardians. Schools and districts may implement different strategies to teach, practice, and reinforce the code of conduct. In maintaining positive behavior, students are expected by the school and district to adhere to the code of conduct and to follow all routines, regulations, and procedures included in the plan.

SUMMARY

School leaders should have an ethical framework that acknowledges that they are acutely aware of the role they play in decision-making. They should be well informed in the area of ethical theories and have the capability to align and apply them to situations and practices. Understanding and making use of ethical frameworks for decision-making will assure fairness and dignity for all school stakeholders. This necessitates adherence to the principles of equity and justice.

The leaders have a duty to recognize the range of dilemmas and conflicting situations that are encountered in their daily interactions with students, families, and community partners. They should have the knowledge and skills to align all policies and guidelines with school-based standards and goals. School visions and values are always aligned with policies. Lastly, sound planning policies should frame all decisions.

School leaders are agents of social and moral excellence who advocate for children and their families. Having personal value systems that generate trust should assist each leader in positively connecting with families and school partners. Creating shared visions that are underpinned with knowledge of policies and procedures can only encourage the success of the school. Handbooks and codes of behavior should advocate policies that can be strictly adhered to by all stakeholders.

CASE STUDY

Mr. White is the principal of South Elementary School. He has worked in that capacity for six months. Mrs. Thompson is the leader of the internal school network. She is well liked by everyone in the school and most teachers seek her advice. She is also a member of most of the social networks in school, and works hard to assist Mr. White as he adjusts to his position. The two of them are presently working on a planning project. The project is due in three days.

Mrs. Thompson was sent out of town by the previous principal during the last school term. She spent five days gathering information that is necessary for the completion of the project. No one else in the school attended the workshop, and Mrs. Thompson did not discuss the training with anyone except the former principal. The former principal was terminated before the start of the year and has not been helpful to Principal White. As a matter of fact, he does not answer his phone calls, nor return his calls.

Principal White was informed three weeks ago that the deadline for the project would be three days from today. However, he was engaged in other projects during the time and did not spend much time working on the project. Besides, Mrs. Thompson told him that it would only take two days to complete the project. They were working alone on the project. The information needed for the project is in Mrs. Thompson's home.

While searching through some files in the office, Principal White found a folder. He opened it to review the content and discovered that Mrs. Thompson spent three years in prison for sexually abusing a neighbors' seven-year-old son. He also saw several correspondences between Mrs. Thompson and the former principal. He discovered from those notes that the sexual abuse information was not shared with anyone else in the district. He also discovered that the former principal and Mrs. Thompson were relatives.

Principal White will not be able to complete the project in three days without Mrs. Thompson's assistance. He waited until now to complete the project because he had confidence they would be able to complete it in the span of three days.

The code of ethics for the district clearly states that no one who has served time for any type of child sexual abuse can be hired in the district. The code also stipulates that anyone having knowledge of that particular infraction must report the incidence or face immediate termination. What should be

Principal White's immediate action? How would the project impact his decision? Discuss his moral obligations to the school and district. Discuss his professional obligation.

EXERCISES AND DISCUSSION QUESTIONS

1. Using the seven-step ethical decision framework in this chapter, discuss the steps Principal White should take to resolve the ethical dilemma.
2. The perception of principals is linked to broader ethical and social issues that include the internal and external opinions and judgments of internal and external stakeholders. In terms of his leadership and mentoring roles, discuss how Mr. White's decision would impact each set of stakeholders: teachers and staff, students, parents, the larger community. How would the stakeholders be affected by Mrs. Thompson's actions?
3. Every aspect of the school's culture is affected by the leadership behaviors of responsibility, performance, and relationship. Use the outcome (final decision) from step seven to discuss Mr. White's moral behaviors associated with responsibility, performance, and relationship.
4. The psychologist James Rest and others present four principles and actions in the development of moral behavior. Write and discuss how this model relates to Mr. White's moral leadership behavior and situation in this case.

REFERENCES

Burns, J. M. (1978). *Leadership.* New York. Harper & Row.

Kohlberg, L. (1973). The Claim To Moral Adequacy of a Highest Stage of Moral Judgment. *Journal of Philosophy, 70,* 630–46.

No Child Left Behind (NCLB) Act of 2001, Pub. L. No. 107–10, § 115, Stat. 1425.

Rest, J., Narvaez, D., Bebeau, M., and Thoma, S. (1999). Postconventional Moral Thinking: A Neo-Kohlbergian Approach. Mahwah, New Jersey: Erlbaum.

Workgroup for Community Health and Development. Chapter 8, (2013). Measuring Progress and Impact of Initiatives. University of Kansas. Retrieved from http://ctb.ku.edu/en/table-of-contents/leadership/leadership-ideas/ethical-leadership/main.

Chapter 2

Ethics, Politics, and Policies

OBJECTIVES

At the conclusion of the chapter you will be able to:

1. Critically analyze, synthesize, and evaluate diverse ethical issues confronting moral leadership in schools (ELCC 5, 6; InTASC 5; ISLLC 5, 6; TLEC 2, 9).
2. Discuss the influence of external and internal conflict on school policy development (ELCC 3, 6; InTASC 7; ISLLC 3, 6; TLEC 7, 9).
3. Understand the leadership needed to educate students from diverse backgrounds (ELCC 2, 5; InTASC 7; ISLLC 2, 5; TLEC 1, 9).
4. Understand the influence of state and federal court decisions and laws on public school programs and operations (ELCC 5, 6; InTASC 7; ISLLC 5, 6; TLEC 9).
5. Discuss some of the legal issues relating to public and nonpublic education (ELCC 3, 6; InTASC 7; ISLLC 3, 6; TLEC 9).

WHEN ETHICS, POLITICS, AND POLICIES COLLIDE

School leadership, power, conflict, politics, and change are closely linked. School leaders make decisions based on the legal, moral, and ethical influences of politics and policies. *Politics* is the use of power to influence decision-making by implementing *policies* and laws in order to control resources. *Power* is the ability to influence, dominate, or control actions. *Conflict* often occurs with a struggle between opposing forces for power. *Change* is the

25

transition from a current state into a future state. Change that alters power relationships promotes conflict.

Federal, state, and local governments influence educational practice by requiring adherence to changing laws, regulations, rules, and policies that motivate and control actions. Many of the government requirements are highly complicated and require school districts to change their processes and structures through policy adjustments. Changes in technology, labor markets, economics, and school demographics can also require changes in school policies. These changes can cause conflict. In brief, the collective needs of society are changing and conflict arises to ensure that schools are managed efficiently.

Public school districts are obligated to uphold laws, regulations, rules, and policies that motivate change and control school governance. This requires changes in policies and school management practices. Importantly, the policies should be adapted to the changes. Achieving positive results related to the changes require strategic planning, communications, research, resolve, policy review, and collaboration.

The dynamics that occur when opposing groups come in conflict are derived from external and internal sources. *External conflict* occurs when external or outside groups or individuals call for substantial changes in district operations. These external groups have targeted goals and agendas for influencing education policy. In many instances, the goals of the external groups may conflict with the district's goals.

Government agencies are often the largest sources of external conflict. The *federal government's* financial contribution to public schooling in America is approximately 9 percent (League of Women Voters of the United States, 2011). While federal funding is minor with respect to total direct elementary and secondary education spending, its role in education policy has increased. Resultantly, many constitutional laws and federal mandates control program planning and policy making in school districts.

The *state* is another governing body that influences external conflict. States have the crucial responsibility for overseeing and safeguarding the operations of public schools. State boards of education are responsible for creating policies that promote educational quality throughout individual states. While the responsibilities of state boards vary from state to state, they are all responsible for maintaining and improving the quality of public schools.

Other groups that are in constant conflict with schools are *politicians, school board members, educational advocacy groups, teacher unions, foundations*, and *corporate groups*. These groups contribute to the national conversation about improving school performance and greater accountability across the educational spectrum. The critical issue for school leaders is the political impact of these organizations on school policy and planning. Figure 2.1 lists a variety of groups that influence education policy.

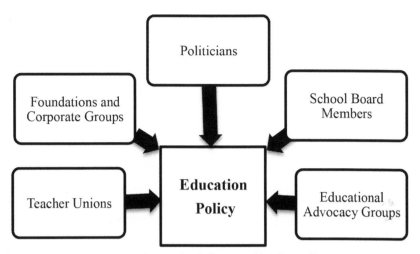

Figure 2.1   Nongovernment groups that influence education policy.

Politicians may have political agendas concerning what is best for the schools. Their agendas may be focused on generating changes that may include limiting or increasing school expenditures or changing the curriculum. Other reasons individuals run for political office may involve issues such as reducing public funding for education, reducing or increasing the role of federal government in schools, and monitoring standards and accountability.

School board members are in power to exercise authority over school districts. They make decisions that impact the lives of educators and students. But their main duty is to establish policies that serve as guides for the daily management of schools. Some of the duties inherent in this position include approving budgets, signing employee contracts, hiring and evaluating the superintendent, purchasing equipment, and managing the collective bargaining process.

Policy analysis and research are the focus of *education advocacy groups*. These groups work to shape policy through aggressive lobbying and campaign activity. Their memberships are often comprised of grassroots organizations that constantly review data and research to inform or influence legislative voting. Some of the issues supported by education advocacy groups include supporting charter schools, closing academically struggling schools, supporting private and parochial schools, and adopting high standards for teaching and learning.

The two most powerful teacher unions are the *National Education Association* (NEA) and the *American Federation of Teachers* (AFT) (Antonucci, 2015). They are both well organized and have powerful voices in education. The main purpose of both groups is to protect the interest of members by supporting candidates who support their beliefs. School-based conflict may largely be due to the fact that the teachers' unions want to be allowed some influence in educational policy making.

Foundations and corporate groups support reform efforts such as deregulation and privatization. Some of the programs they support are privately managed charter schools, vouchers, tax credit for scholarships to private schools, union-busting tactics, and the curriculum. Private foundations spend billions of dollars annually to support or transform K-12 schools (Urban Institute, 2012). Grant writing is a key approach that foundations and corporate groups use to fund schooling (Rajan and Tomal, 2015).

Internal conflict occurs when stakeholders from within schools and districts form individual or political structures. Those stakeholder relationships form for a variety of reasons and come from *formal* and *informal organizational structures* within the school. These stakeholders have the capability of influencing learning environments. Realistically, they can produce pressures in the internal environments of schools and districts and stimulate change.

The *formal organizational structures* are the ones depicted in the organizational charts or hierarchy of schools and districts. Some examples of formal groups are district-level school leaders, school-level department members, specific school grade levels, school and district committee members, and advisory board members. In the formal organization, the emphasis is on official positions or titles. Members of formal groups usually work in accordance with written sets of rules, policies, and procedures.

Conflict can arise in the formal school organizational structure when leaders of formal groups are coercive, autocratic, or rigid. Examples would be grade-level committee chairpersons who do not accept input from group members who have similar experiences and skills. These leaders can dampen morale, reduce group productivity, and cause internal school conflict. Also, some of the committee members may try to dominate meetings and push their own agendas. Both situations can cause internal school conflict.

The *informal organizational structure* is made up of individuals with similar behaviors and value systems. Informal practices are defined by the patterns, behaviors, and interactions that stem from personal relationships. Individuals in this group may lead or direct without an official leadership title. This may be particularly true in schools that have experienced repeated layoffs and budget shortfalls. Conflict in the informal organizational structure may develop when the opinions of some individuals regarding curricula, teaching practices, and school policies differ from that of the school leader.

Effectively managing internal conflict is an important leadership responsibility. It involves the encouragement of open communication and being available to teachers, parents, students, and staff. The bottom line is that school leaders should work collaboratively with faculty and staff to provide policy, curricula, and instruction that enhance positive learning environments. Some of the leadership activities in this process include:

- Monitoring external and internal environments for early threats of change.
- Facilitating and modeling effective communication.
- Expressing value for dissenting views.
- Administrating proactive planning for the implementation of needed changes and strategies.
- Promoting generative thinking and involving educators in ways that promote opportunities throughout the school.
- Incorporating multidimensional leadership roles for the staff.
- Influencing followers to take ownership in generating new ideas.
- Increasing the quality of decision-making among staff.

School leaders are constantly adjusting policies to meet the demands of external and internal political and social forces. This is accomplished through changes in school and district policies. The policies should ensure that both students and teachers will learn, develop, and adapt to the changes. This will involve the alignment of the school curricula with strategic policies and plans that are undergirded with successful teaching and learning supports.

THE INFLUENCE OF STATE AND FEDERAL
COURT DECISIONS AND LAWS

School districts are supported by multiple state and federal initiatives that provide funding and programs to assist in educating students. The purpose of the system-wide government support is to promote educational goals and programs needed to educate and prepare students for citizenship and society. Control over financial interests in schools provides governing agencies the power to influence and control the manner in which schools are governed.

The general approach federal, state, and local governing agencies use to promote changes in educational policies is to focus on *standards-based teaching and learning*. Standards-based teaching and learning is directed by predetermined state standards for learning that require school districts to design plans for instruction that link learning standards with desired outcomes and goals. This means that the school leaders should ensure that viable curricula are delivered through evidence-based instructional strategies. Most important, standards-based teaching and learning should require that high-quality professional development be provided to all educators.

The standards movement is arguably a major force in education today. Recently, the New America Foundation (2014) reported that Americans spend over $550 billion a year on public elementary and secondary education in the United States. All three levels of government contribute to that funding. Reasonably, the education community is being pushed by these governing agencies to provide all students with high-quality, comprehensive education.

Understanding the *standards-based reform movement* requires a brief history of public education in America. Historically, education was chiefly private and funded by families and religious groups until Massachusetts passed the first compulsory school laws in 1852. Before that time, social and family status dictated how much education a person received. By 1918 all states had some form of compulsory school attendance laws (U.S. Department of Education, 2010). This was the inception of public schools in America.

Supporters for public schools called for more centralization and bureaucratic control and asked the federal government to take a larger role in overseeing education on a national level. In an answer to this appeal, the federal government appropriated $15,000 to create the Department of Education in 1867. The Department of Education was later changed to the Office of Education. The major responsibility of this agency was to collect and distribute statistics on education in America (U.S. Department of Education, 2010).

The Department of Education has established itself as the creator of *standards-based teaching and learning*. The agency's name and location within the Executive Branch have changed over the past 130 years. However, the early emphasis on getting information on what works in education to teachers and education policy makers continues to the present. Presently, assessing what works in schools is driven by the setting of academic standards for what students should know and be able to do in grade- and course-level classrooms.

When school systems were first formed, in most states teachers were mandated to teach reading and writing as tools for promoting religious values. Currently, public school teachers are required to have a bachelor's degree, be fully certified, and demonstrate subject-matter knowledge through testing and other accountability measures. Many states have created programs for midcareer changers and others who have content knowledge to be certified through alternative routes. The programs are required to offer high-quality professional development, as well as intensive and structured ongoing support (Learning Point Associates, 2007).

The landmark Elementary and Secondary Education Act of 1965 (ESEA), passed during President Lyndon Johnson's presidency, became the core of federal K-12 policy. The Individuals with Disabilities Education Act subsidizes resources and programs such as school technology, teacher training, student literacy, and textbooks. Between 1965 and the early 1990s, the federal education role consisted of categorical education programs designed to address specific issues such as high-poverty schools and non-English-speaking populations.

Standards-based accountability began with Goals 2000 during the Clinton administration. Goals 2000 was enacted to set goals for outcome-based standards reform. The aim was to measure improvement in student achievement across all groups. This standards-based education reform was the beginning of a new era in school and education reform.

President George W. Bush increased federal involvement in schools with the enactment of the NCLB. This act was the restatement of the ESEA and is the largest source of federal spending on elementary and secondary education. The purpose of the act was to raise achievement for all students and to close the achievement gap among groups of children. This was done through state accountability standards, standards-based curriculum frameworks, research-based instruction, and tests aligned with mastery-based instruction.

The increasing involvement of state and federal government in supporting new standards-based policies and mandates in schools began a period of changing perspectives of policy on public education. The change requires a balance between new government mandates and traditional school practices. Significantly, standards-based reform represents a structural shift in the way state and federal policies and school practices are framed. Standards-based reform requires links between the state's responsibility for setting accountability and assessment targets, the district's responsibility for designing curricula and assessment policies, and increased achievement targets for all students.

As a result of NCLB, district curriculum assessment and policy changes include information and guidelines that should help teachers plan standards-based units and lessons to ensure students learn grade- or subject-level content. Every teacher should ensure that students' learning is linked to the mastery level. A variety of instructional strategies and knowledge of students' learning needs are essential for mastery-level learning. The result should be improved academic achievement.

School districts respond to state accountability and assessment mandates by designing new curricula and assessment policies. This requires them to set objectives, agree on action plans, and allocate resources for policy frameworks and programs. The changes include focusing on test preparation, altering instructional strategies, and making changes in classroom assessment practices. These policies should ensure that tests are aligned with high-quality instructional practices in all classrooms.

There are times when no policy can be developed to meet government mandates. The reason is that mandated programs do not always deliver enough money to meet the cost of program implementation. These are called *underfunded mandates*. An example of an underfunded mandate is the Individuals with Disabilities Education Act.

IDEA is commonly referred to as the special education law. The law requires that students with disabilities cannot be denied special education services due to lack of funding, personnel, or other resources. This means that school districts must meet and accommodate special needs students, regardless of the cost. In some districts this requires transferring funds from other school accounts into the IDEA program.

Another IDEA example of an unfunded mandate is state caseload limitation for special education and gifted teachers. The most common special education caseload mandates are based on a combination of factors. Some of the factors include the presence of paraprofessional educators, age or grade of students, educational setting, type of service, disability category, and the severity of the disability. Federal laws governing services for students with disabilities do not contain any specific requirements for caseload or class size.

Another unfunded mandate imposed upon teachers and school leaders in many states is the requirement for certification extensions. All fifty states require educators to take additional course work or training, regardless of their present certification status. The requirement is the reaction to NCLB, which compels states to have *highly qualified teachers* in every classroom. Highly qualified teacher requirements apply to all teachers who teach in the core academic subjects.

Unquestionably, teacher subject-matter knowledge is associated with student learning. Amrein-Beardsley (2012) analyzed the work of over twenty researchers on the topic of teacher quality and concluded that highly qualified teachers are "the single-most important school-level factor related to increases in student achievement" (p. 9). In this era of high standards and high expectations, school leaders must make every effort to fill vacant teaching positions with highly qualified teachers. This requires that policies and procedures be in place to ensure all teachers meet requirements.

NAVIGATING DIVERSITY ISSUES

Interest in the ethical and moral leadership role of the school leader is of paramount importance in today's society. This interest is related to the changing dynamics and complexities of the twenty-first century. Schools are becoming more demographically and ethnically diverse. As a result, school districts are enrolling increasing numbers of students whose cultural and linguistic diversity is a challenge to school leaders, staff, and other students.

In 2012, the Center for Public Education (CPE), an initiative of the National School Board Association (NSBA), reported results from research conducted on demographic changes and student enrollment in public schools. The results show that the youngest populations are the most diverse and that 21.6 percent of children under age 18 live in poverty. The research also determines that 47 per cent of children younger than five belong to a racial or ethnic minority group. Significantly, the report discovered that nearly 20 percent of the students aged five and older speak a language other than English at home.

A report in 2014 from the Children's Defense Fund (CDF) concurs with the research findings from CPE. Additionally, the CDF research investigated the age demographics of student populations and determined that the majority of children in America under age two were children of color. Further, CDF predicts that by 2019 the majority of all children nationwide are expected to be children of color. These trends should have important implications for school leaders, policy makers, parents, and the community at large.

Those findings suggest that the hiring of bilingual teachers and teachers of English language learners will be urgent requirements of the twenty-first century. The findings also imply that early childhood interventions may be critical in reducing the disparity of the students' home lives. Leaders in these schools can work actively to bridge the gaps that may hinder parent support. Some of the activities they undertake may involve providing parent training and involving parents in decisions affecting the education of their children.

Discussion of diversity in our public schools should involve community stakeholders. Many schools and districts develop comprehensive outreach strategies and engage parents and community members in planning and goal setting. This should require the deliberate advancement of policies and actions that recognize commonalities and differences among groups. These will ensure that internal and external school stakeholders understand the purpose and rationale behind diversity-related goals.

It goes without saying that school leaders should hold high standards for themselves and others. If they are culturally competent school leaders, they will institutionalize cultural practices that should assure that teachers acquire the attitudes, knowledge, skills, and dispositions needed to work effectively with all students. The practice involves having a *focus on vision and purpose, staff training, collaboration* and *team building*, and *building consensus*. A caring and nurturing diverse school environment and culture will be the outcome. Table 2.1 summarizes cultural practices and potential outcomes of caring, diverse school environments.

Having a *focus on vision and purpose* drives personal behavior. Staff and students become motivated for success when leadership shares vision, enthusiasm, and purpose-driven learning goals. This practice aligns all stakeholder actions with the values and goals of the school. Inviting classrooms and learning conditions are the results.

Staff training is essential for creating learning conditions that meet the needs of all students. The training can assist educators in understanding how to work with students of diverse backgrounds. This will allow the staff to

Table 2.1 Cultural practices and potential outcomes of caring diverse school environments

Cultural Practices	Potential Outcomes
Focus on vision and purpose	Stakeholders' actions are aligned with school values and goals.
Staff training	The staff recognize cultural behaviors and respond appropriately.
Collaboration and team building	Teachers gain encouragement as they learn about each other and share teaching ideas.
Building consensus	Allows input from all stakeholders into the decision-making process.

recognize cultural behaviors and respond appropriately. The outcomes should be caring learning environments for both teachers and the students.

Collaboration and *team building* help educators who work with the students to meet together and talk about curriculum issues, instructional strategies needed to meet the diverse learning needs of all students, and ways to form authentic and caring relationships in diverse classrooms. This relationship assists in having a shared sense of culture. Teachers are also able to gain encouragement as they get to know each other and share teaching ideas. Moreover, collaboration and teaming should provide supportive environments in which no one in the school feels alone and isolated.

Building consensus allows school stakeholders to work together to seek mutually acceptable resolutions of complex school issues. Building consensus also allows input from all stakeholders in the decision-making process. Importantly, building consensus helps to establish a framework for developing solutions that work for everyone. Students perform well in environments where school stakeholders work together to form collaborative and caring environments.

Parent support is also essential. It may be important that teachers invest some time in getting to know students and their families. Teachers can send letters to parents to introduce themselves. The letters may include classroom expectations, curricula goals, and invitations to parent meetings and other classroom and school activities. This information will also assist parents in understanding their roles in meeting the educational needs of their children. Figure 2.2 lists several school-wide diversity strategies that schools can use to enhance the parent-school relationship.

THE RESULT OF STATE AND FEDERAL LAWS

Challenging schools to prepare students to compete globally is increasingly becoming a major role of the federal government. Local government agencies

Begin the school year by using a parent survey to determine needs of the students and their families.

Provide at least two parent meetings for the year. Focus the meetings on the responses from the surveys.

Discuss the school vision and mission at each parent meeting.

Provide information regarding the instructional programs during both meetings.

Provide bilingual services to parents with limited English-speaking proficiencies.

Use the school's website for daily communication with families.

Use various platforms to intermittently communicate with parents, including emails, school newsletters, and webinars.

Provide information that informs how parents can assist the students at home.

Invite parents and community members to sign up for memberships in various committees.

Figure 2.2   School-wide diversity strategies and practices that enhance parent-school relationships.

as well as local advocate groups are also raising national and community awareness of the need to provide educational opportunities for all students. Additionally, educators, policy makers, and educational researchers are disseminating information on what they believe works best in schools. The result of all this information is that all Americans should be concerned about building and sustaining quality in pre-K through 12 education.

The role of state government influence over schools is not uniformly prescribed throughout the country. This is because states have different constitutional laws, educational policies, and executive acts. Each state has absolute authority to govern the education of students within its borders. Powers may be explicitly delegated or merely implied.

Charter schools are public schools that are independently allowed to operate with more flexible outcome goals than traditional public schools. These schools offer parents the opportunities to choose educational environments that they believe are appropriate for their children's education. All charter schools receive state funding. Some charter schools provide programs for students who struggled in traditional public school settings.

Nonpublic or *private schools* may be independent or secular, or provide religious instruction as part of their curriculum. Nonpublic schools that are religious in nature are usually called parochial schools. Parents and guardians of compulsory-school-age students have the legal right to enroll them in nonpublic schools. Nonpublic schools have fewer legal obligations to abide by constitutional law.

Homeschooling provides an educational setting where children are educated at home instead of in traditional public or nonpublic schools. All fifty states allow parents to homeschool their children. State requirements for homeschooling vary from state to state. The National Center for Educational Statistics reported in 2012 that approximately 3 percent of the school-age population was homeschooled in the 2011–2012 school year.

No two states regulate nonpublic schools in exactly the same way. However, nonpublic school students in all states are entitled to some publicly funded services, which are either provided by the school district in which the student resides or the district within which the nonpublic school is located. These services are limited to, but not inclusive of, health and homebound services, computer software, resources from the school library, and special education services. Nonpublic schools have more accountability to parents than public schools.

All U.S. public school districts are required by state laws to have compulsory school attendance policies (National Association of State Boards of Education, 2015). These attendance policies should stipulate requirements for attendance from kindergarten registration to graduation. Nonpublic schools are also required to create, maintain, and keep attendance records of students.

Most states also require that immunization records be maintained for all students.

While states have absolute power in the area of education, they must not violate the provisions of the U.S. Constitution. Such was the case when families of the Old Order Amish religion and the Conservative Amish Mennonite Church were convicted of violating the Green County Wisconsin school district's compulsory school attendance law (Wisconsin v. Yoder, 1972). Wisconsin compulsory attendance law requires that students remain in school until age 16. The Amish religious groups believe that having their children remain in school after age 13 would be detrimental to their salvation.

Jonas Yoder, the father of one of the students, maintained that the application of the compulsory school attendance law violated the rights of Amish communities to raise their children. Yoder argued that Amish communities provide informal vocational education to their children on an ongoing basis. His assertion was that the informal vocational education prepared the students for life in their Amish community.

The Green County Wisconsin Court found the Amish community guilty and fined them five dollars. Yoder took the case to the Wisconsin State Supreme Court. The Supreme Court found that the state's compulsory school attendance law violated the Amish way of life under the Free Exercise Clause of the First Amendment. The school district appealed the case to the U.S. Supreme Court. The U.S. Supreme Court ruled in favor of Yoder in a unanimous decision (Wisconsin v. Yoder, 1972).

The U.S. Constitution recognizes the rights of public school students. The Constitution and its amendments, statutes, and rules govern how schools operate. Many of the laws and policies related to racial segregation, religious rights, due process, freedom of speech and expression, school choice, and unreasonable searches and seizures have been addressed by the federal court system.

The federal judicial system has played an essential role in establishing educational policy in public schools. There are several amendments that directly influence the operations of schools and districts. They are the *First, Fourth, Fifth,* and *Fourteenth Amendments*. The relationships of these amendments and school governance are discussed in the following passages.

The *First Amendment* (U.S. Constitution, Amendment I) addresses the right of individuals to act on and express their religious belief. The amendment also guarantees freedom of speech in schools. This freedom may include the freedom to dress, protest, and express political opinion, within reason. This means that the right to free speech must be conducted in ways that do not interfere with the educational mission of the school.

The *Fourth Amendment* (U.S. Constitution, Amendment IV) addresses the rights of students to be free from unreasonable searches and seizures.

How school leaders conduct a search of students and their property is subject to the protection of this amendment. There are circumstances and situations in which a search of student property is warranted. Student and school safety is included in this category. In order to provide a safe and secure environment for all students, many public schools use various forms of search, including mass search of the entire student body, metal detectors, random drug testing, and strip searches.

The *Fifth Amendment* (U.S. Constitution, Amendment V) addresses the idea of fairness and protects against self-incrimination. This means they cannot be forced to testify against themselves when charged with offenses. Additionally, school leaders must give the students and staff the opportunity to hearings. Leaders must also provide the evidence necessary to substantiate the charges.

The *Fifth Amendment* (U.S. Constitution, Amendment V) also requires that students and staff be afforded their due process rights for charged offenses. Due process requirements stipulate that detailed information regarding charged offenses is provided to the students or staff members being charged. The accused individuals must be given an opportunity to respond to the charges. If due process is not followed, any penalty that is given can be reversed.

The *Fourteenth Amendment* (U.S. Constitution, Amendment XIV) addresses the *Equal Protection Clause* that prohibits school districts from treating people differently. The Equal Protection Clause requires that students with disabilities have the same opportunity to receive a free and appropriate (suitable) public education as students without disabilities. The Equal Protection Clause also requires that schools not discriminate on the basis of disability. Parents also have due process rights related to how their children are to be educated.

IDEA (2004) has provisions that oversee how public school districts provide early intervention, special education, and related services to nonpublic school students with disabilities who live within their districts. The legal rights of nonpublic school students and the responsibilities of public school district administrators are specifically defined by IDEA.

In particular, local public school districts must provide specific services to nonpublic school students within their districts. These services include the provision that all referred nonpublic school students be evaluated to determine if they are eligible for special education. If the students are eligible for services, the public school district must develop an appropriate *Instructional School Plan* (ISP) for the student. Importantly, the public school district must consult with parents and the student's teachers when developing an ISP.

IDEA (2004) continues to require that public school districts only have to provide special education services to students in nonpublic schools if the district has referred or placed the student in the setting. This act also stipulates that students who are placed in nonpublic schools by their parents do not have the right to receive some or all of the special education and related services that they would receive if enrolled in a public school.

This may be a concern for nonpublic school parents. For example, a district may agree to provide a nonpublic ISP autistic student 60 minutes of special services per week. At the same time, the district can choose to end the services for the nonpublic school student if funding runs out during the school year. However, if the student were enrolled in the public school, five days of special education support would be provided.

The basis of the concern is that IDEA only requires public school districts to spend a portion of their federal special education funds on students with disabilities in nonpublic schools (IDEA, 2004). This allocation is called "proportionate share." The amount allocated for nonpublic schools is usually much smaller than the overall funding the district is given to spend on students who attend schools in the public school district. In some cases, and if the students' disabilities are limiting their educational progress, parents have the right to enroll them in the local public school district. In this case, the students would receive all of the mandated IDEA services.

DISTRICT CODES OF ETHICS

Codes of ethics are written guidelines and rules that outline social norms that govern proper practice in organizations. Specifically, codes of ethics link organizational missions, values, and principles with standards of professional conduct. Further, codes of ethics outline the guidelines and procedure used to determine consequences, limits, and sanctions. Adhering to the guidelines of codes of ethics should be a requirement of all members and stakeholders.

School boards provide local control of school districts by providing conduct standards in the form of codes of ethics. Local control refers to the governing and management of public schools that are located in the communities served by school districts. District codes of ethics should outline the guiding principles and expected behaviors for district stakeholders who are under the control of local school boards. Importantly, the codes of ethics should ensure that students are educated in environments that are conducive to teaching and learning, and free of disruptive conduct.

While school boards are described as having local control of districts, oversight by state boards of education on school districts places significant limitations on school board actions. For example, state-governing structures set basic codes of ethics that provide governance, oversight, and limitations on school districts within each state. State laws and standards support these state codes of ethics. Local school boards within each state are obligated to design district codes of ethics that align with state educator codes of ethics.

Most important, the codes of ethics should be supplemental to state and local laws, rules, and regulations and not conflict them. The districts' codes of ethics should be written and applied to all stakeholders, including board members, employees, guests, and school district volunteers while on school property. Violations may incur administrative or disciplinary actions up to and including suspension, dismissal, or other actions as required by law.

School leaders are responsible for maintaining effective learning environments. Codes of ethics are key tools in enabling the school leaders to carry out those responsibilities. The leadership standards that define these responsibilities include maintaining professional relationships with school stakeholders, avoiding conflicts of interest, and not accepting gifts or compensation for personal gain. Other leadership standards include careful maintenance of funds and school properties, the ethics of confidentiality, and avoiding appearances of impropriety, including refraining from the use of alcohol, tobacco, or drugs (see table 2.2).

Ethical school leaders should maintain professional relationships with all students and make their educational success a priority. Respecting the dignity and worth of students should be a required standard in all state codes of ethics. The state codes should also require that district curricula designs be based on high expectations for all students. For example, the Illinois Educator Codes of Ethics requires that Illinois districts design, implement, and adapt individualized instruction that meets students' needs (Illinois State Board Advisory Group, 2014).

Another example is the Georgia Professional Standards Commission (2014), which requires that all educators maintain professional relationships with students at all times. The commission describes some conducts related

Table 2.2   Leadership standards and conduct requirements in district codes of ethics

Standards	Required Conduct
Maintain professional relationships	Assure that the environment is safe and efficient for student learning.
Avoid conflicts of interests	Ensure that professional duties are not influenced by personal interests.
Do not accept gifts, favors, gratuities, or compensation	Ensure that school policies and procedures are followed when receiving gifts from outside sources.
Maintain confidentiality	Guarantee the privacy of student and district personnel records.
Account for public funds and properties	Provide procedures and oversight for all funding and business accounts.
Do not use alcohol, drugs, or tobacco	Avoid using alcohol, tobacco, or controlled substances during professional practice.

to the standard that are viewed as unethical. These include soliciting, encouraging, or consummating inappropriate written, verbal, electronic, or physical relationships with students. The commission defines unethical conduct as "including but not limited to the commission or conviction of a felony or of any crime involving moral turpitude; of any other criminal offense involving the manufacture, distribution, trafficking, sale, or possession of a controlled substance or marijuana" (p. 1).

Conflicts of interest in school districts take place when personal responsibilities and interests influence educational leaders' professional duties or responsibilities. These conflicts of interests may include family relationships, memberships in community groups, and business involvements. For instance, conflicts of interests may occur when school leaders use district resources for personal or community use. Conflicts of interests may also exist when family members or acquaintances of school leaders receive favors as a result of their relationship with the school leaders.

School leaders should not accept *gifts, favors, gratuities,* or *compensation* for personal gain. Importantly, codes of conduct should ensure that school policies and procedures are not impacted by gifts or gratuities from individuals or organizations. However, school leaders in Illinois are permitted to receive monetary gifts from individual sources that have a total value of less than $100 in a calendar year (Illinois Council of School Attorneys, 2014, p. 1). The Illinois Council of School Attorneys also stated that school leaders were permitted to use district funds to purchase food, in an amount not exceeding $75 in a single day, while attending meetings away from the district (p. 2).

Conversely, the code of ethics for the Chicago Board of Education (2011) permits school leaders to receive gifts, money, or honoraria for participating at official out-of-district speaking engagements. However, the leaders are required to report the payment to the chief financial officer within ten business days of the engagement. Accepting compensation for out-of-district services unrelated to the leader's official duties is also permitted.

A vital responsibility of school leadership is to ensure that the *confidentiality* of students and district personnel records and other information covered by confidentiality agreements is exercised. Significantly, and unless a disclosure is required by law, the records must be kept in complete confidentiality. Equally important is the maintenance and security of students' health records and family status. For instance, the Georgia Professional Standards Commission (2014) forbids the sharing of records related to students' health or family status.

Educational leaders are entrusted by states and school districts with *public funds and property*. These leaders should honor that trust with high levels of honesty and responsibility. Importantly, the school leaders should have systems in place that account for all funds collected from all school or district stakeholders. It is vital that the use and record keeping for all school resources meet state and federal laws and regulations. For example, the Ohio State Board of Educators (2011) lists several "unbecoming" behaviors by school leaders related to public funding:

- Failing to account for funds related to school activities collected from students, parents, family members, community members, staff, or peers in accordance with local board policy.
- Comingling public or school-related funds with personal funds or checking accounts.
- Submitting fraudulent requests for reimbursement of expenses (p. 5, 6).

Lastly, the *use of alcohol*, *tobacco*, or *drugs* during the professional practice is restricted. School leaders are responsible for creating standards of exemplary conduct. Creating those standards begins when the leaders engage in behaviors that encourage ethical conduct. Examples of unethical school leadership behaviors cited by the Georgia Professional Standards Commission (2014) include:

- The school leaders are on school or district premises or at school-related activities involving students while documented as being under the influence of, possessing, or consuming alcoholic beverages.
- The school leaders are on school or district premises or at school-related activities involving students while documented as using tobacco or tobacco products (p. 2).

SUMMARY

Students come to school from diverse backgrounds and cultures. Ethical school leaders are responsible for working with school stakeholders to develop and articulate a common vision that promotes student achievement throughout schools and districts. These leaders should respect the values of every member of the school. They should have strong commitment and concern for the education of all students, and believe that every student can succeed. These leaders should also work with internal stakeholders to create learning environments that promote trust, collaboration, and professional growth. In addition, these leaders should support student empowerment and work to build strong relationships with parents and external stakeholders.

In order to respond to political, demographic, social, and legal challenges from external and internal stakeholders, ethical school leaders should take the initiative to invite external stakeholders to assist in planning and policy development. Ethical leaders should also understand the importance of open communication with internal stakeholders. The input received from stakeholder relationships should assist in strengthening school policies. Likewise, the leaders should periodically review their own performance.

It should be the duty of all school leaders to place a high premium on ethical behavior. School leaders are responsible for influencing ethical practices and behaviors in schools and districts. Furthermore, school leaders should be committed to providing quality educational experiences for all students.

School leaders, through the use of a district code of ethics, can set conduct standards throughout the district. Codes of ethics should define professional standards of conduct and acceptable behaviors. The codes of ethics should also define unethical behaviors for which disciplinary actions are justified.

CASE STUDY

Mrs. Chatman moved into District 108A in July. Her son, Steven, had previously attended a nonpublic school that was located in the vicinity of a large urban school district. While attending the nonpublic school, Steven received full services for autism from the large urban public school district.

District 108A is a rural district and has limited special education funding. Three weeks after moving into the district, and six weeks before the start of school, Mrs. Chatman met with the coordinator of special education, Mrs. Rogers.

Mrs. Chatman informed Mrs. Rogers that Steven would need services for autism. She also told Mrs. Rogers that Steven would be attending a private school that was located in the area. She further stated that Steven had been provided full special education services by the large urban school district he left.

Mrs. Rogers informed Mrs. Chatman that District 108A had limited funding and Steven would not be able to receive full service for his disability unless he attended a public school within the district.

- Discuss how Mrs. Rogers and Mrs. Chatman should work together to ensure that Steven maintains all of his special education rights and services.
- Research the reauthorized IDEA of 2004 to determine legal requirements.

EXERCISES AND DISCUSSION QUESTIONS

1. How are states and districts held accountable for improving teacher quality? Why is this issue so important?

2. What challenges do changing demographics and diversity issues present to teachers?
3. Discuss the role of the school leader in navigating diversity issues in schools.
4. What has been the role of federal courts in regulating public school education?
5. How are state requirements for traditional public schools and charter schools different? How are they alike?
6. Design a code of ethics for your school district or community organization and center it on the following leadership duties: maintaining professional relationships, avoiding conflicts of interests, abstaining from appearances of impropriety, and careful and informed management of fiscal resources.
   - What process will you use to create a code of ethics?
   - Who will be involved?
   - How will the code of ethics be implemented?
   - How will it be publicized and disseminated, both inside and outside of your school district?
   - How and when will the code of ethics be reviewed and revised?

REFERENCES

Amrein-Beardsley, A. (2012). Recruiting Expert Teachers into High-Needs Schools: Leadership, Money, and Colleagues. Education Policy Analysis Archives, Retrieved from http://epaa.asu.edu/ojs/article/view/941.

Antonucci, M. (2015, Winter). Teachers Unions and the War Within: Making Sense of the Conflict. Education Week, Retrieved from http://educationnext.org/teachers-unions-war-within/.

Center for Public Education. (2012). *The United States of Education: The Changing Demographics of the United States and their Schools.* Alexandria, VA.: Retrieved from http://www.centerforpubliceducation.org/You-May-Also-Be-Interested-In-landing-page-level/Organizing-a-School-YMABI/The-United-States-of-education-The-changing-demographics-of-the-United-States-and-their-schools.html.

Chicago Board of Education. (2011). *Code of Ethics for the Chicago Board of Education.* Retrieved from http://policy.cps.edu/download.aspx%3FID%3D32.

Children's Defense Fund. (2014). *The State of America's Children.* Washington D.C. Retrieved from www.childrensdefense.org.

Elementary and Secondary Act of 1965. Retrieved from http://www.gpo.gov/fdsys/pkg/STATUTE-89/pdf/STATUTE-89-Pg773.pdf.

Georgia Professional Standards Commission. (2014). *The Code of Ethics for Educators.* Atlanta, GA. Retrieved from http://www.gapsc.com/Rules/Current/Ethics/505-6-.01.pdf.

Illinois Council of School Attorneys. (2014). *Prohibited Illinois Association of School boards: Answers to FAQs Regarding the Gift Ban Provisions of the State Officials and Employee Ethics Act* {Brochure}. Retrieved from https://www.iasb. com/law/COI_FAQ.pdf.

Illinois State Board Advisory Group. (2014). *The Illinois Educator Code of Ethics.* Illinois State Board of Education. Retrieved from http://www.isbe.net/prep-eval/ pdf/meetings/emag/pdf/educator_COE_0311.pdf.

Individuals with Disabilities Education Act Amendments of 1997. Retrieved from https://www2.ed.gov/policy/speced/leg/idea/idea.pdf.

Individuals with Disabilities Education Act of 2004. Retrieved from http://www. parentcenterhub.org/wpcontent/uploads/repo-items/IDEA2004regulations.pdf.

League of Women Voters of the United States. (2011). *The Education Study: the Role of the Federal Governments in Public Education.* Retrieved from http://lwv.org/ content/role-federal-government-public-education-equity-and-funding.

Learning Point Associates. (2007). *Understanding the No Child Left Behind Act: Quick key 6, Teacher Quality.* Retrieved from http://www.learningpt.org/pdfs/ qkey6.pdf.

National Association of State Boards of Education. (2015). *State Boards of Education.* Retrieved from http://www.nasbe.org/about-us/state-boards-of-education/.

National Center for Educational Statistics. (2012). *Household Education Surveys Program of 2012.* Retrieved from http://nces.ed.gov/pubsearch.

New America Foundation. (2014). *Federal Education Budget Project: Background and Analysis.* Retrieved from http://febp.newamerica.net/background-analysis/ school-finance.

No Child Left Behind Act of 2001. Retrieved from http://www2.ed.gov/nclb/landing. jhtml.

Ohio State Board of Education. (2011). *Licensure Code of Professional Conduct for Ohio Educators.* Retrieved from http://education.ohio.gov/Topics/Teaching/ Educator-Conduct/Licensure-Code-of-Professional-C.

Rajan, R., and Tomal, D. (2015). *Grant Writing.* Lanham, MD: Rowman & Littlefield Education, Inc.

Urban Institute. (2012). The *Nonprofit Section in Brief: Public Charities, Giving, and Volunteering, 2012.* Washington, D.C. Retrieved from http://www.urban.org/ research/publication/nonprofit-sector-brief-public-charities-giving-an.

United States Constitution. Amendment I.

United States Constitution. Amendment IV.

United States Constitution. Amendment V.

United States Constitution. Amendment XIV.

United States Department of Education. (2010). *Thirty-five Years of Progress in Educating Children with Disabilities through Idea.* Retrieved from http://www2. ed.gov/about/offices/list/osers/idea35/history/idea-35-history.pdf.

Wisconsin v. Yoder, 406 U.S. 205 (1972). Supreme Court of the United States.

Chapter 3

Making Haste Slowly

Politics at the District and Board Levels

OBJECTIVES

At the conclusion of the chapter you will be able to:

1. Describe the roles and functions of a school board (ELCC 1, 2, 3, 4, 5, 6; InTASC 1, 3, 6, 9, 10; ISLLC 1, 2, 3, 4, 5, 6; TLEC 1, 2, 3).
2. Identify potential problems among board, district, and school leaders (ELCC 2, 3, 4, 5, 6; InTASC 1, 3, 6, 9, 10; ISLLC 1, 2, 3, 4, 5, 6; TLEC 1, 2, 3).
3. Identify how politics impact the diverse needs of students (ELCC 2, 5, 6; InTASC 6, 9; ISLLC 2, 5, 6; TLEC 1, 2, 3, 6, 7).
4. Describe the role of policy and politics in district governance (ELCC 2, 5, 6; InTASC 6, 9; ISLLC 2, 5, 6; TLEC 1, 2, 3, 6, 7).
5. Describe community involvement in district politics (ELCC 2, 5, 6; InTASC 6, 9; ISLLC 2, 5, 6; TLEC 1, 2, 3, 6, 7).

HISTORICAL CONTEXT OF SCHOOL BOARDS

What is the role of school boards in public education? It is likely that in every community there are differences of opinion about the purpose of the community's *public schools*. The word "public" in public school refers to the fact that it is the citizens themselves who control the public schools. In most states, depending on the size and configuration of the district, they do this by electing a school board of three, five, or seven members, who must be residents of the school district.

According to recent data from the U.S. Department of Education, school boards govern the overwhelming majority of the approximately 13,600 school districts in America and they make up fully one-sixth of all the local governments in the country (U.S. Department of Education, *Digest of Education Statistics*, 2012, table 216.20). School boards also retain broad popular support. They are how citizens have been accustomed to seeing their school districts governed for the past century and the means through which parents and community members gain access to school policies and procedures.

Local control over education forms a core value in the foundation of our nation. To understand the potential influence of local school boards, it is important to look at their authority within the context of state and federal education policy. Dating back to the founding of our nation, public education has been the responsibility of the state. This function was granted through the tenth amendment to the U.S. Constitution.

This article states, "The powers not delegated to the United States by the Constitution, nor prohibited by it to the States, are reserved to the States respectively, or to the people (U.S. Const., article X)." Since education is not mentioned in the Constitution, it is one of those powers reserved to the states. Thus, states have *plenary*, or absolute, power in the area of education.

In turn, states have delegated this responsibility to locally *elected school boards* charged with overseeing the operations of specific schools. Over time, this responsibility has evolved to the oversight of clusters of schools organized under the administrative umbrella of central district offices guided by state-specific education policies and codes, which are also influenced and governed by federal statutes. So, it is not a surprise that elected school boards are a legacy of our origins as a nation.

Supporters of this governance model see local school boards as an essential reflection of our commitment to representative democratic government and local control. Yet, there are many contemporary critics who dislike them and see them as a hindrance to both equity and quality in education. Critics cite a history of low expectations, inequitable funding, and segregation by race and economic status as evidence that local control can lead to organizations that do not reflect our broader national values or commitment to equal opportunity for all citizens.

Beginning in the 1960s, and building on arguments made in *Brown v. Board of Education*, 1954, the federal government began playing an increasing role in public education through federal legislation and categorical funding such as the ESEA amended in 2011, and the Education for all Handicapped Children Act of 1975 (EHCA). Both of these laws were designed to provide resources to students marginalized in school systems largely due to policies developed by state and local school boards (e.g., policies that segregated students by race, disability, income, or funding that led to substantial inequities).

Subsequent Congressional reauthorizations of ESEA, EHCA, IDEA, and NCLB further expanded the role of the federal government. These acts make funding available to districts to provide additional support for specific groups of students (e.g., students with disabilities and students living in poverty). The influential NCLB and associated regulations target persistently low-performing schools and support initiatives such as the *Common Core State Standards* aimed at ensuring that all states strive to teach a high level of curriculum and administer rigorous assessments.

POLICY AND THE SCHOOL BOARD

Under these conditions with local control seemingly eroded by more and more federal oversight, what then is the evolving role of the school board? The NSBA states, "School board members serve their local communities as stewards of public trust charged with making decisions that ensure all students have access to high quality learning experiences in efficient and well managed environments" (NSBA, 2011, p. 2).

The NSBA developed a framework of eight critical areas called the *"work of school boards"* that school boards may adopt in order to be effective in improving student achievement. While not intended to be addressed in any specific priority order, NSBA suggests the areas are to be considered and implemented as a whole to create optimal conditions for student success (see figure 3.1 for the NSBA's eight key work areas of school boards).

The foundation for these important key work areas is called *policy*. Policies are principles adopted by school boards to chart a course of action. They may include why and how much is needed for the initiatives taken. Policies should be broad enough to indicate the procedures to be followed by the district leaders in meeting a number of problems and narrow enough to give clear guidance. Policies are guides for action by the board of education, which sets the rules and regulations so as to provide specific directions to school personnel.

Boards develop policies and put them in writing so that they may serve as guidelines and goals for the successful and efficient functioning of the public schools. Most school boards consider policy development their chief function, along with providing the guidelines for actions concerning personnel, buildings, resources, and equipment for the successful administration, application, and execution of their policies. Policies serve as sources of information and guidance for all people who are interested in, or connected with, the

1. Identify vision and mission
2. Develop standards for performance
3. Support assessment of performance
4. Implement accountability for performance
5. Align resources to support performance
6. Prioritize climate and culture
7. Develop collaborative relationships and engage community
8. Commit to continuous improvement

Figure 3.1 Eight key work areas of school boards. *Source: National School Board Association, www.nsba.org, 2011.*

public schools. It should be noted that policies of school boards should be framed, and interpreted, in terms of laws, rules, and regulations of the state boards of education, and all other regulatory agencies within county, state, and federal levels of government.

The following represents a sample policy development process that a school board may adopt and use to formulate guidelines and structure for the governance of the schools under its jurisdiction (see figure 3.2):

1. A new policy or update is identified.
   Required changes or an additional policy noted by the following:
   a. Board (including approved board resolutions and/or board policy committee studies, reviews, and recommendations)
   b. Superintendent
   c. Legal requirement or local county, state, or federal mandate
2. Superintendent (or designee) studies issues and prepares abstract/policy development guidelines.
   This defines issues and suggests approaches to be taken.
3. If one exists, the board subcommittee charged with policy development reviews potential policy development guidelines and develops a position.
   This subcommittee suggests a position on issues, agrees on scope, establishes policy priority schedule and implementation guidelines.
4. Superintendent prepares a working or first draft.
   Legal counsel is consulted if necessary and/or required.

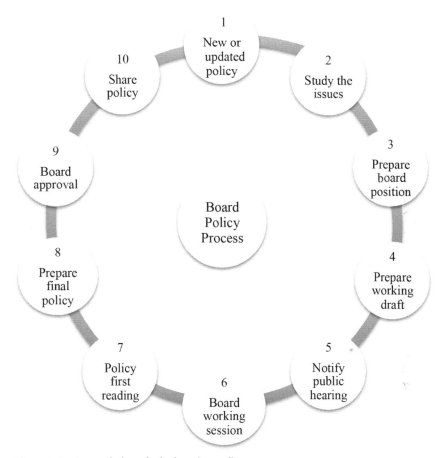

Figure 3.2 A sample board of education policy process.

5. Announcement and distribution/notification of a proposed new or revised policy as an agenda item on a regularly scheduled board of education meeting.
6. Board reviews draft during a board working session.
7. Board reviews draft at first reading in a regularly scheduled meeting. *Board members agree on substance and suggest wording change, if necessary.*
8. Superintendent prepares final policy statement.
9. Board takes action on the policy at second reading in a regular scheduled board meeting.
10. When approved/adopted, superintendent distributes and shares the policy.

In most districts, the superintendent is directed to establish and maintain an orderly plan for preserving newly adopted policies and making them accessible to employees of the school district, to members of the board, and to the community at large. It is now common practice that an updated board of education operating policy manual is kept in electronic format through the district's web page. Also, a copy of the updated policy manual is normally filed with the state commissioner or superintendent of education. As policies are added, deleted, or amended, a notice of each policy is kept on file on the district website and a copy filed with the state education office.

It is common practice that at least every two years, a board will review its policies for the purpose of passing, revising, or deleting policies mandated by changing conditions. Boards should evaluate how the school staff has implemented policies. The board should rely on the school staff, students, and/or the community to provide evidence of the effect of the policies adopted. The superintendent is delegated the responsibility of calling to the board's attention all policies that need revision.

The following criteria may be used when evaluating policies for possible revision or updating as required by law or mandate:

- Is the policy within the scope of the board's discretionary authority granted by state codes and statutes?
- Is the policy consistent with state and federal law and with the provisions of the U.S. Constitution or existing federal statues?
- Does the policy have a legitimate purpose that is educationally valid and/or have a desirable end or objective?
- Does the policy reflect sound judgment and wisdom?
- Is the policy in the best interest of children or adults it affects?

Legal counsel should always be sought, when in the opinion of the superintendent or the board, a question exists regarding the legality of a policy.

POLITICS AND THE SCHOOL BOARD

Now that we have established the context for boards of education, let's explore the politics that affect the efficient operation of a board and the school district. It is important to identify two important principles concerning school boards as they affect school and district leaders working with these boards. These principles are:

1. All school and district leaders are agents of the board of education, and as such, are required to carry out board policy and procedures; and

2. All school and district leaders must have a clearly developed personal moral and ethical framework as they work with boards of education.

These statements may seem simplistic and obvious to any leader. However, these two principles are critical to the success of school board operations, district governance, and administrative performance. The three unknown dynamics influencing all parties involved are those of *politics, control, and power.*

Many issues drive the politics of local school districts and their boards. These influences could include but are not limited to: 1) level of community participation in school board elections both in terms of voter turnout and in terms of challengers to incumbent board members, 2) community demand for change influencing school board policies, 3) polarization and partisanship of community, county, state politics leading to evidence of partisanship on school boards, and 4) board member personal agendas as reason to seek election to a school board.

For a theoretical foundation of the politics in community school boards, studies that began in the 1970s cited the development of several theories of the role of school boards in making educational policy influenced by politics. These schools of thought, drawing on larger theories of democratic representation and politics, are summarized as *dissatisfaction theory, continuous participation theory, and decision-output theory.* A fourth theory, *public choice theory,* emerged in the early 1980s.

Dissatisfaction Theory describes an electoral system with relative stability and little involuntary incumbent turnover punctuated by periods of extreme citizen dissatisfaction, contentious elections, and incumbent defeats (Iannaccone and Lutz, 1970; Lutz and Iannaccone, 2008). If one ignores nonpolitical cases of board turnover, such as voluntary retirements, poor health, or a family move out of the district, then *Dissatisfaction Theory* can generate some useful predictions.

Alsbury (2008) makes the case that, in order to evaluate how responsive school board elections are to democratic forces, it is necessary to conduct a study of many districts over several electoral cycles. However, *Dissatisfaction Theory* provides very little insight into the motives of board members, superintendents, and voters.

Changing school board policy requires an inactive electorate to activate, challengers to run to replace incumbents in favor of the status quo, and a majority of board members to be defeated or change their positions in response to the voter will. This most often leads to a change in the school district superintendent. *Dissatisfaction Theory* does explain aggregate outcomes, such as turnover of school board members that leads to turnover of district superintendents. It does not explain the motives of candidates to run

Table 3.1   Theories of school board and community politics

Theory	Description	Key authors
Dissatisfaction	Long periods of stability in board elections interrupted by short periods of high turnover and participation.	Iannaccone and Lutz, 1970 Lutz and Iannaccone, 2008
Continuous Participation (Competition)	The small percentage of voters who continuously participate in board elections have their preferences accurately reflected. Any spikes in participation are in line with the wishes of these interest groups.	Zeigler et al., 1974, 1978
Decision-Output (Responsiveness)	The undemocratic nature of school boards stems from the limited policy scope that board elections control, namely, the public can only vote on local tax revenue and the policy makers on the board (who are constrained by federal and state laws, statutes, and policies).	Wirt and Kirst, 1989 Hess and Meeks, 2011
Public Choice Theory	Challenges to incumbents arise based on policy choices of board members, voter preferences, and the expected payoffs associated with policy change.	Rada, 1988, 1987 Moe, 2005, 2011

for the school board or of voters to vote for challengers, other than to say they do so out of dissatisfaction with the direction of the district. Thus, the political motives of board members, voters, and candidates are masked in such a theory.

Continuous Participation Theory argues that policies and political turnover in local districts are largely misleading. The basis of this theory argues that any changes in the makeup of the school board or in the school board policies represent a true change in the preferences of 5–10 percent of the electorate who are constantly involved in educational policy at the local level. Spikes of participation may occur, but they are the direct result of the actions of this small group of active citizens. As a result, the decisions that result from such periods of greater participation are in line with the views of the citizens that have been engaged all along.

A study in 2011 conducted by Moe researching educational policy making at the local level by teachers' unions can trace its roots to this theory. He argues that teachers' unions function as a local interest group in educational policy making driving everything from school board candidate emergence, to voter turnout, to selection and replacement of district superintendents.

Thus, when voter participation spikes or challenger candidates emerge, it is not a reflection of broad dissatisfaction within the community, but of a concentrated effort to activate the electorate on behalf of the goals of the local interest group.

A third theory, *Decision-Output Theory*, is a derivative of *Continuous Participation Theory*. It argues that educational policy at the local level is largely undemocratic. However, policy is undemocratic not because of capture of the system by a single interest group, but rather because the electoral inputs available to citizens allow them only to determine who makes public policy and how much local tax revenue to raise in support of schools (Wirt and Kirst, 1989).

Citizens are not able to truly determine education policy in these circumstances, but merely to determine the constraints within which educational policy makers must operate. In fact, it is the unelected and appointed district superintendent that dominates policy making due to informational advantages and professional training. This often reduces the issue dimensions in a school board election to a single fiscal dimension. In such elections, the vote asking to raising tax levies and making new capital investments does not permit citizens to decide on the substantive content of the curriculum of study available to the community's students.

Finally, *Public Choice Theory* is a later arrival to the study of school district governance. This theory borrows heavily from a *rational choice* background often viewed in economics and political science. In application to school boards, two types of school board members emerge, the *power* and/or the *prestige candidate*. *Power candidates* seek positions on the school board to change district policy and make decisions. *Prestige candidates* seek a position to fulfill civic duty or to gain notoriety within the community. Applying this single dimension (power or prestige) to board members generates a number of expectations about the emergence of different types of candidates, electoral challenges, and policy changes within a community.

All four of the theories have deep roots in political science literature. Understanding school boards provides an opportunity to evaluate what democratic policy making looks like across a wide spectrum of citizen participation. While variations exist in state and federal Congressional district elections, school board elections provide a much wider spectrum playing an influential and often contentious role in communities. Additionally, boards are a fascinating test of candidate emergence. Entry to school board office is relatively inexpensive and most often completely free of party affiliations, unlike legislative office. It is why so many community members seek the office, when often, the only qualification they have is living within the school board boundaries.

Critics of school boards have a long and legitimate list of grievances. Turnout in school board elections is often quite low, making it easier for special interests (groups with single-focus ideological agendas or factions interested mostly in steering contracts to themselves and their friends) to get candidates elected. In many places, the very nature of school board politics seems to draw people with axes to grind, rather than motivated community leaders. There are many examples of communities where board members are in conflict with the district polices and politics. They're supposed to be setting policy for the school district, but they themselves are in conflict with each other and the policies they are attempting to disseminate.

Even when they are able to put ideology, partisanship, and personal gain aside, school boards today face an overwhelming set of challenges: federal laws on special education and the new assessment and racial reporting requirements imposed by NCLB; federal court decisions on the rights of religious groups and the need to accommodate students with disabilities; state laws setting academic standards, advancing charter schools and reshuffling of school finances; and negotiations on union contracts that govern pay scales, class sizes, teacher assessment, hiring and firing procedures.

All of these fall into the laps of school board members. That's in addition to choosing and monitoring a superintendent, opening and closing schools, approving or disapproving charters, making decisions on buying or selling property, or formulating and then trying to sell bond measures to the voters. Effective district governance is not easy. It is time-consuming and can be a thankless job at best. Into this mix, we include people who often have no background in finance, administration, consensus building, political leadership, or even education. These are critical skills that the job of a school board member practically demands. There are some states that require training for new members, but even then it is often cursory or quickly forgotten in the turmoil of meetings and decision-making.

The political excesses of elected school boards around the country in recent years have been the primary factor driving some cities toward a radically different approach. That approach is direct mayoral control of the schools with all or most of the board members serving by mayoral appointment. For example, the mayors of Boston, Chicago, New York, and Oakland have all put such systems in place.

However, mayoral control may not be the answer. It doesn't work everywhere. But the right circumstances, such as being able to appoint a majority of the board, having a city and school district that are coterminous, and having a mayor who actively wants to improve the education of the children in the city, may make a difference.

Although the system of mayoral control and appointment has shown itself to be promising in some cities, the fact still remains that the vast majority of school board members in America are elected, and will continue to be. So the question is whether an elected board, in a troubled system badly in need of reform, can do what is needed to change the system.

POLITICS AND MEETING THE DIVERSE
NEEDS OF STUDENTS

It is not difficult to argue making it a priority to educate each and every American child. We read continuously in newspapers and see on television and computers about the urgency associated with closing achievement gaps and in eliminating the disparities in the educational attainments of different races and classes so that all children can learn. Local school board elections are one place where citizens can make a difference, and where the dialogue can begin. Through technology, innovation, and strategic public involvement, board members may be able to move schools to becoming more competitive with other industrialized nations.

To create optimal conditions for student outcomes, local boards must understand how their macro-level decisions impact principals, teachers, and students, and then align resources accordingly. Heavily influencing school districts are federal and state statutes and mandates that play a role in shaping local policy. For example, while curriculum decisions have historically been made at the local level, they are increasingly being influenced by state and federal policy as seen in the initiatives of the *Common Core State Standards* and federal *NCLB flexibility waivers* designed in large part to introduce rigorous standards nationwide and improve student outcomes.

The literature examining the correlation between school board actions/ policies and student outcomes is limited and needs updating. Nevertheless, a seminal multiyear *Lighthouse Inquiry Project* conducted by the Iowa School Boards Foundation from 1998 to 2000 documented a correlation between student achievement and the actions and beliefs of board members that has potential relevance. The original study and subsequent follow-up projects demonstrated that particular school board actions and beliefs transfer to district personnel and lead to better student outcomes even in high-poverty districts. Specifically, the *Lighthouse study* found the following board characteristics present in high-performing, high-poverty districts, and missing in low-performing, high-poverty districts:

• Inspiring versus accepting belief systems (e.g., board members see schools as raising students' potential as opposed to seeing students' potential as fixed);

- Focusing on continuous school renewal and increased student performance (e.g., board members understand school improvement and change processes); and
- Action planning in schools and classrooms (e.g., board members are knowledgeable about school improvement plans (SIPs) and action planning processes).

The *Lighthouse study* is important in school board research because it documented the correlation between school board attributes, actions, and student outcomes.

A more recent study from the NSBA focused on school board actions in developing diversity polices and the need to address learning for all students. This study actually followed up the NSBA's collaborative role in the *Lighthouse study*. The 2011 NSBA study is entitled *Achieving Educational Excellence for all: A Guide to Diversity-Related Policy Strategies for School Districts*. This well-researched and reflective study states in the foreword, "Our hope is that leaders at all levels of the school community, from school board members to educators, to superintendents and parents, use this resource to move the conversation forward about the importance of diversity as a means for achieving educational goals, and that they do so in a way that is not only legally sound, but also reflects the best values of the communities they serve" (NSBA, 2011, p. 5).

This study uses recent research data and demographics to present a clear case that now is the time to meet the needs of our diverse learners. We cannot wait decades more because time is not on our side. The snapshot provided by this study of our national student population is a telling piece of data collection. Several highlights from the NSBA snapshot reveal that:

- By 2050, racial and ethnic minority groups, who have the lowest rates of high school and college completion, will comprise 55% of the working-age population in America.
- Roughly two of every five black or Hispanic students attend segregated schools (in which 90–100% of students are minorities), up from less than one-third in 1988, while 8% of white students attend schools with 50–100% minority student populations.
- Segregation tends to be multidimensional with corresponding levels of socioeconomic and language isolation. More than 80% of segregated black and Hispanic schools are poverty concentrated, while only 5% of white schools are indicated as poverty concentrated.
- Economically and racially isolated schools result in limited student access to opportunity networks for employment and postsecondary education.

These schools generally provide fewer educational offerings and resources and have higher teacher turnover and lower teacher quality.

- Diverse schools produce educational and lifelong benefits, enhancing civic values, improving student learning and preparation for employment, and increasing educational opportunities. Diverse schools provide students with deeper ways of thinking, higher aspirations, and positive interactions with students of other races and ethnicities. These are life experiences that translate into positive, long-term benefits for living and working in diverse settings (NSBA, 2011, p. 11).

While school and district performance is influenced by complex internal and external factors, school board members are positioned to make a difference. Of note, the study points out that individual board members' belief systems shape their decisions and actions which influence the quality of schools. Furthermore, board members' level of knowledge of the schools and the initiatives designed to improve student learning can make a difference in outcomes. The challenge for board members is to obtain enough knowledge to make informed decisions, while guarding against using this knowledge to micromanage the superintendent and district staff.

School Board Training and Student Performance Outcomes

To be effective managers, and specifically to initiate, support, and sustain targeted school improvement efforts (e.g., turnaround schools), local school board members require a clear understanding of their role in district governance and knowledge about what changes are required to improve schools. Training provides school board members opportunities to learn about their key roles and responsibilities, as well as more substantive content related to education policy and practice.

In an NSBA study in 2010 focused on mandated board training, it was found that twenty-three states require school board members to obtain training with varying levels of prescription, rigor, and compliance. The state of Maine, for instance, requires new board members to participate in a single, two-hour orientation about freedom of information laws, while Texas requires new board members to complete at least sixteen hours of training, specifies the focus (e.g., initial district orientation, orientation to state education code, and team building), and requires that experienced board members complete at least eight hours each year.

In New York, newly elected members are required to complete six hours of training regarding fiscal oversight and governance skills. Of the states that require training, most allow the state school board association, as well as other approved external vendors, to provide such training.

Requirements, however, only have meaning if the training is of high quality, compliance is tracked, and there are consequences for noncompliance. For example, it is important to establish language that permits the state to bar members from running for reelection, if they have not completed their required training. Holding up compliance with the training requirement as a criterion for reelection may introduce a degree of accountability to the process. However, adequate research has not been conducted regarding the actual impact of training requirements or the consequences of failure to fulfill the training requirements.

Implementing Diversity Policies in School Districts

In the decades following the 1954 *Brown v. Board of Education* decision, school districts continued to focus on resolving problems of the past and acting to end segregation of students on the basis of race, income, and disabilities. The most intensive period of school desegregation occurred from 1968 to 1972. During this period, the percentage of black students in severely segregated schools dropped dramatically.

Later U.S. Supreme Court cases established scope and time limitations for these remedial policies. Once a district established that it no longer operated separate school systems for white and nonwhite students, it had satisfied the remedial purposes of the courts' desegregation order.

Yet, school districts are not required to exercise desegregation policies forever. Legally mandated racial integration has significantly less relevance to districts now than in decades past. Much of district energy today focuses on the educational, community, and economic benefits that can result from well-developed board policies and strategies that are mission focused, results driven, and student directed.

This reflects a major shift in how education leaders think and act about diversity issues. Although legal issues are never far removed from the conversation, this shift reflects a move from an externally imposed set of legal duties required by courts or federal agencies to correct for past wrongs to institutional choices.

Against this historical perspective, districts must ensure that diversity policies are developed as tools to promote educational benefits in learning and not to achieve diversity for its own sake. By doing so, boards can ensure that they are on solid footing both legally and practically. Refer to figure 3.3 for a sample process for developing a diversity policy.

Addressing Diversity in School Districts

Diversity can be defined as a multifaceted view that acknowledges, validates, and celebrates the richness of our human similarities and differences.

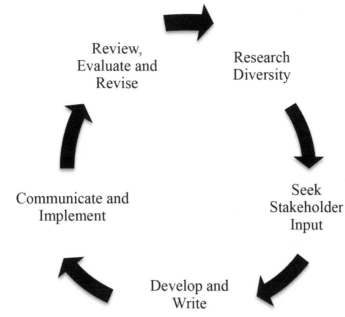

Figure 3.3 A diversity policy process.

Given the ambiguity of the term and the frequent debates that surround diversity, it is important that school boards define their diversity policy with sufficient clarity. Properly understood, the term "diversity" need not always mean code for race, ethnicity, or gender alone. While a school board's concept of diversity may include these factors, the policy should be far more comprehensive. It should include relevant qualities and experiences that influence learning in and out of the classroom reflecting the community served.

When addressing diversity in a student population, multiple factors should be considered. Many district policies include, in addition to race, ethnicity, and sex, references to socioeconomic status, neighborhood, language status, special education needs, academic performance, record of achievement, community engagement or interest, and much more.

For example, a school district may assign students to schools based on parental choice, which may include a diversity index of the student's neighborhood (determined by the racial, socioeconomic, and adult education levels of neighborhood residents). The board could also include priority categories that relate largely to the proximity of their school of choice and siblings attending the school of choice. For assignment to small, specialized district programs, the assignment policy may also take into account special education and English language learner status.

In another scenario, student assignment factors might include parental choice, geographical proximity to school, and a diversity index that measures socioeconomic status, academic achievement, home language, and extreme poverty of individual students. Yet another school district's interdistrict student assignment policy could reflect consideration of parental choice, residential address, race, behavioral history, and special education status.

Also, the board's concepts of student diversity do not have to be static. For example, diversity goes beyond traditional classifications such as white, black, or Hispanic to include giftedness, socioeconomics, primary language, special learning needs, and culture.

As these examples make clear, a district's definition of diversity should not reflect a one-size-fits-all model, but one that includes specific educational goals and student needs, with consideration of family history and community beliefs. Ultimately, diversity policies should be framed around the unique educational needs of students, not around maintaining certain legalistic numerical population targets.

POLITICS AND THE COMMUNITY

No serious discussion of diversity in our schools can or should take place without community involvement. Perhaps more than any other governmental entity, school boards and their decisions directly influence a community's citizens. This role places boards of education, district and building leaders, teachers, and support staff in a prime position to enlist the input and support of parents and community leaders in a variety of issues, including advancing a district's diversity goals. Community engagement and outreach requires that school boards carefully frame conversations about a diversity-related policy like student building assignment so everyone understands its purpose, rationale, and substance.

For instance, the building of new schools and the drawing or redrawing of attendance lines may elicit strong public sentiment and comment centering on proposed board actions that affect personal interests. But this issue presents an opportunity for the board to lead the community by shifting the conversation to one about diversity as an educational value to the school district and the community.

When well established, diversity policies should be pursued to advance larger educational goals such as realizing higher student achievement, preparing students to be competitive in a global economy, and developing civic and democratic values. School boards must be clear about these larger goals, ensuring that district educators and community members fully understand the purpose and rationale behind any diversity-related policy.

This means helping the public understand that diversity programs are not necessarily remedial intending to correct past wrongs, or about racial balancing, affirmative action, or special benefits to a particular group. Rather, diversity can be about providing academic and educational benefits to all students, resulting from the uniqueness of a diverse student body, that acknowledge and celebrate student similarities and differences.

School boards and school leaders routinely engage the public in a variety of ways, and many of those avenues of communication become opportunities for carrying out the diversity conversation. Many districts conduct regular workshops and hearings with specific time slots on their agendas asking for citizen input. In fact, because state laws often govern local policy making, many boards must conduct public hearings before policies are formally adopted.

In policy development, boards often rely on citizen advisory committees, with members providing both lay and professional perspectives that can prove invaluable.

Community and business leaders are important voices in the discussion, often offering potential solutions that enrich the public debate and highlight the importance of diversity to the business community. Citizen advisory committees, especially when a school board is addressing controversial policy areas, can help reduce tensions and garner support.

In 2010, the Boston Public Schools faced a challenge when leading civil rights groups charged that the district was not engaging the community about its student assignment process. The groups' recommendations to improve engagement included creating a task force to address specific challenges, involving community organizations and local foundations in the diversity dialogue, and expanding media awareness. All of those suggestions are methods that districts nationwide could use.

Ultimately, boards can employ various means to pursue diversity-related goals that are aligned with evidence-based educational goals. Conversations around these issues will become part of the record in a legal challenge. Consequentially, the terms used and the purposes stated in meetings (including public meetings) are particularly important because they can demonstrate the board's intent. If questions arise about racial balancing in a discussion, those supporting a particular student assignment policy must be able to disprove racial balancing as a motivation. This shows the board's real focus was not on providing benefits based on race, but rather on student achievement goals.

Considering a new or revised policy, such as a student assignment plan, requires a carefully deliberated process of evaluation. In other words, boards should carefully study and research to ensure the plan's success and sustainability. Ultimately, diversity-related policies must be developed using a transparent process that is understood by everyone.

Before establishing or refining a policy, a school board should gather relevant information about its context and history. This exercise may take weeks, months, or, for some large districts, even a year or two. Specifically, the board should examine district demographic information (including race and socioeconomic status), any governing court orders, relevant local or state laws, the educational effects of any current or previous assignment plans, and political structures. Also, a board should give substantial consideration to community values and interests. Public outreach can and should be informed by the background information you collect, and school boards should anticipate criticisms by preparing persuasive responses and by developing a consistent public message.

Finally, districts must periodically review and evaluate the design and operation of policies to ensure they are achieving the desired results. Periodic review is legally necessary for all policies. More so for diversity policies because this ensures that any consideration of race and ethnicity continues to serve interests in appropriately personalized ways. Boards must ensure that diversity policies always reflect the educational goals of the district and of the community.

Boards should look at diversity-related policies every few years. Working with an interdisciplinary team of key district officials, knowledgeable staff, experts in research and evaluation, and lawyers, the board should examine all relevant data, including student demographics and academic achievement over time. The outcome is to determine whether the policy is having its intended effect. Also, key district leaders should talk to other school districts that have tried different methods.

Boards should hold public hearings and be receptive to public feedback from the community as well as from students and families. They should consider whether other design options would be as or more effective at achieving the district's goals, and document the board's rationale for discarding alternatives where appropriate.

Ultimately, a school board must ensure that the goals of the diversity policy are reflected, complemented, and reinforced in the classrooms and hallways. Boards must work with schools to support their diverse student populations through curricular and extracurricular offerings and student services that create a culture in which student difference is acknowledged and celebrated.

POLITICS AND SCHOOL LEADERS

As stated earlier in this chapter, district and school leaders are heavily influenced by the politics in the community and district they serve. They are legally and contractually bound to the policies and procedures of the board of education. Therefore, it is imperative that district and school leaders carefully study board policies and community politics. It is equally important that they understand and respect the values and culture of the community they serve. This may challenge personal beliefs and values. What is a leader to do?

First, the leader must have established a *personal belief system* built on a solid moral and ethical foundation. Secondly, the leader must have a clearly articulated *conceptual framework* built on relevant and principled leadership theories. This framework should reflect best practices in educational leadership and reflect high ethical standards of personal conduct.

Not only must these standards be internalized in the leader, but they also must be evident in the day-to-day actions the leader takes in the district and school. Leaders can get caught between what is practical and seemingly right in the circumstance, and a school board policy or procedure that may need changing or updating. But most often, leaders are simply caught in the micromanagement of board members who may have personal agendas.

These personal agendas have a profound effect on and influence leader behaviors and actions. For example, a school leader may be caught in a situation where a board member's child has violated the school discipline code. The school leader must take required board policy action and administer the appropriate consequences. However, the board member intervenes and demands that the student action be ignored and/or dropped. Is it politically expedient to ignore the student behavior, or is it best to "let the chips fall where they may"?

Take for example, a case where parents, students, and community members challenge a board policy and administrative actions. For instance, a very popular teacher has been accused of poor behavior and possible student abuse. Board policy requires that the district and school leader investigate and take appropriate action concerning the student and the teacher. In this case, the district leader, supported by the school leader, suspends the teacher in question. There is outrage in the community, student protests, and a grievance filed by the union on behalf of the teacher. What are the district and school leader to do in this situation?

The case cannot be discussed in public as it violates the rights of the student and the teacher in question. The press and community cannot be briefed as it could violate due process. Such are the political realities of dealing with board policies concerning teacher discipline. The district and school leaders in this case must judiciously navigate a fine line between protecting the student and teacher while supporting board policy and managing the fallout from the situation. It requires administrative actions that are balanced and well rooted in an ethical and moral framework.

Take another situation that could easily happen to any district or school leader. The board is persuaded to take employee disciplinary action due to bias against the leader voiced by a member(s) of the board, community, or students. Such politically motivated actions may lead to dismissal and possible lawsuits. Leaders must be aware of the possibilities of such actions by boards.

They should always have in place the protection of a legally binding written contract and personal conduct rooted in moral and ethical behavior supported by fair and equitable actions. Consequences of board actions based on bias or unsubstantiated personal allegations can lead to mistrust, anger, recriminations, and power struggles. District and building leaders must remember they are agents of the board, but they must also balance this principle with a personal value and belief system that ultimately is supported by transparent actions, words, and deeds.

SUMMARY

This chapter reviewed the role of school boards in the public school educational process. Evidence was presented to show that school boards are one of the closest democratically elected entities to the community. School boards provide a wide array of services and assistance to the community. Citizens gain access to school district services and initiatives through board politics and practices. Yet, what becomes evident in communities across America is the impact that politics plays on the governance of local school districts.

The increasing role of the federal government was referenced in such federal laws as ESEA amended in 2011, EHCA, IDEA, and NCLB. Local control of education seems to erode with such initiatives as the *Common Core State Standards*. It appears more and more federal oversight is challenging boards across the nation, especially in the area of student diversity.

Studies were cited that shed light on the critical role boards have in establishment of diversity policies in the public schools. Board policy development was highlighted to illustrate how boards can impact the day-to-day instruction of all learners. We learned that boards must work with communities to support their diverse student populations and help create school cultures and climates in which student differences are acknowledged and celebrated.

The chapter also focused on the conflicts within district and school settings that could occur between leaders and boards of education. Leaders must create a balance between their own personal beliefs and values and the beliefs and values of the citizen-elected board of education. When conflict does occur, district and school leaders need to rely on a strong ethical framework supported by a relevant conceptual framework of leadership theory.

CASE STUDY

You are a high school principal of 2000 students. Your school has a very successful and active athletic program with wide community support. The program is guided by a board policy with a written Student Athletic Code of Conduct. All students who participate in any athletic program must sign this code of conduct and have it countersigned by parents. This code is kept on file by the school athletic director.

During the winter break, the athletic director approved a meeting at the home of the head coach of the girls' varsity volleyball team. In attendance were the head coach and her assistant coach and the entire varsity team. The athletic director informed you that it has come to his attention that alcohol was available to the students and coaches while in attendance at this meeting. The school board policy is clear and specific where alcohol is concerned: if found to have been drinking in violation of the code, students must be suspended pending a disciplinary hearing and are barred from practices and playing in any athletic contest for the remainder of the semester.

Further, there must be disciplinary action taken with the coaches. Board policy requires that the coaches be suspended as well until the incident is investigated and resolved. The local newspaper has gotten the story and printed it as headline news in the community. You have already suspended the students, and recommended to the superintendent that the coaches in question be suspended with pay pending board hearings. The superintendent has supported your recommendations and taken the necessary actions.

As you drive to school one morning you observe student and community members surrounding your school with protest signs in support of the team and coaches. You notice that the local news outlets are there with cameras as well. What steps will you take to protect your suspended students and teacher rights? What steps will you take in the investigation process? How will you support the board policy when one of the players is a child of a board member?

EXERCISES AND DISCUSSION QUESTIONS

1. Research the McKinney-Vento homeless act and discuss how this federal law impacts the policies of a school district and the day-to-day operations of the school.

2. Research the policies of your school district concerning student attendance center assignment. Is your district policy fair and equitable for all students? What would you change or alter, if needed? Why? What is missing in the policy?

3. Does your school district have a board policy for bullying? Cyberbullying? If not, what language might a policy like this contain?

4. Research the student discipline code of your district. Does your discipline code have a policy concerning appropriate technology use to include cell phone or other personal electronic uses in the school and classroom settings?

5. Research your district board policy on ethics and conduct. Does the policy apply to board members as well as all school district employees? If not, what might the policy language contain? If yes, explain how it is fair and equitable to all parties involved. Would you change the policy in any way to improve it?

REFERENCES

Alsbury, T. (Ed.). (2008). *The Future of School Board Governance: Relevancy and Revelation.* Lanham, MD: Rowman & Littlefield Education, Inc.

Alsbury, T. (2003). Superintendent and School Board Member Turnover: Political versus Apolitical Turnover as a Critical Variable in the Application of the Dissatisfaction Theory. *Educational Administration Quarterly, 39,* 667.

Brown v. Board of Education, 347 U.S. 483 (1954).

Common Core State Standards Initiative. (2015). Retrieved from www.corestandards.org.

Delagardelle, M. L. (2008). The Lighthouse inquiry: Examining the Role of School Board Leadership in the Improvement of Student Achievement. In T. Alsbury (Ed.), *The Future of School Board Governance: Relevancy and Revelation.* Lanham, MD: Rowman & Littlefield Education, Inc.

Education for all Handicapped Children Act of 1975. Retrieved from https://www.govtrack.us/congress/bills/89/s773.

Elementary and Secondary Education Amendments Act of 2011. Retrieved from https://www.govtrack.us/congress/bills/112/s1571.

Hess, F., and Meeks, O. (2011). School Boards Circa 2010: Governance in the Accountability Era. Washington, DC: National School Boards Association.

Iannaccone, L., and Lutz, F. (1970). *Politics, Power, and Policy: The Governing of Local School Districts.* Columbus, OH: Charles E. Merrill Publishing Company.

Individuals with Disabilities Education Act of 1997. Retrieved from https://www.govtrack.us/congress/bills/104/s1142.

Iowa Association of School Boards. (2000). The Lighthouse Inquiry: School Board/Superintendent Team Behaviors in School Districts with Extreme Differences in

Student Achievement. Paper presented at the American Association of Research, 2001 Annual Meeting.

Lutz, F., and Iannaconne, L. (2008). The Dissatisfaction Theory of American Democracy. In T. Alsbury, (Ed.), *The Future of School Board Governance: Relevancy and Revelation* (pp. 3–24). Lanham, MD: Rowman & Littlefield Education, Inc.

Moe, T. (2005). Teacher Unions and School Board Elections. In J. Howell, Besieged: *School Boards and the Future of Education Politics.* (pp. 254–87). Washington D.C.: Brookings Institution Press.

Moe, T. (2011). Special Interest: Teachers Unions and America's Public Schools. Washington D.C.: Brookings Institution Press.

National School Board Association. (2011). Achieving Educational Excellence for all: A Guide to Diversity-related Policy Strategies for School Districts. Alexandria, VA: Author.

National School Boards Association. (2010). Mandated Training for Local School Board Members Survey. Retrieved from www.nsba.org.

National School Boards Association. (2011). What School Boards Need to Know: Data Conversations. A Report for Schools Boards in Planning for and Using Data Systematically. Alexandria, VA: Author.

National School Boards Association. (2012). Content Related to Effective Board Governance. Retrieved from: www.nsba.org.

No Child Left Behind Act of 2001. Retrieved from https://www.govtrack.us/congress/bills/115/s1425.

Rada, R. D. (1987). An Economic Theory of School Governance. In Annual Meeting of the American Educational Research Association.

Rada, R. D. (1988). A Public Choice Theory of School Board Member Behavior. *Educational Evaluation and Policy Analysis, 10*(3), 225–36.

Rada, R. D., and Carlson, R. (1985). Community Dissatisfaction and School Governance. In Annual Meeting of the American Educational Research Association.

U.S. Constitution. Article. X.

U.S. Department of Education, National Center for Education Statistics. (2013). *Digest of Education Statistics, 2012* (NCES 2014-015), Chapter 2.

Wirt, F., and Kirst, M. (1989). *The Politics of Education: Schools in Conflict* (2nd ed.). Richmond, CA: McCutchan Publishing Corp.

Zeigler, L., Jennings, M., and Peak, W. (1974). *Governing American Schools: Political Interaction in Local School Districts.* North Scituate, MA: Duxbury Press.

Zeigler, L., and Tucker, H. (1978). Responsiveness in Public School Districts: A Comparative Analysis of Boards of Education. *Legislative Studies Quarterly, 3*(2), 213–37.

Chapter 4

Leading from the Front

Politics in the School Building

OBJECTIVES

At the conclusion of this chapter you will be able to:

1. Describe the political relationship between administration and teachers and its effect on school life (ELCC 1, 3, 6; InTASC 3, 9, 10; ISLLC 1, 3, 6; TLEC 1, 2, 3, 7).
2. Describe the political relationship between administration and noncertified staff and its effect on school life (ELCC 1, 3, 6; InTASC 3, 9, 10; ISLLC 1, 3, 6; TLEC 1, 3, 6, 7).
3. List and describe critical factors to reduce politics within the school building leadership team (ELCC 3; InTASC 3, 9, 10; ISLLC 3; TLEC 1, 3, 6).
4. Describe the various leadership styles and their effect on school politics (ELCC 3; InTASC 3, 9, 10; ISLLC 3; TLEC 1).

POLITICS AND TEACHERS

The Greek statesman Pericles warned, "Just because you don't take an interest in politics, doesn't mean it won't take an interest in you." As a school leader, it might be easy to declare that politics has no place in the discussion of teaching and learning. Such a declaration would be both noble and naive because it fails to recognize that those who work in schools, like those in most organizations, seek some *control* over their work.

Politics is the practice of *influencing* people. In highly effective schools, teachers and leaders embrace a *shared responsibility* for student achievement and success. Leaders are tasked with leading schools, while teachers lead students in their classrooms. For the teacher and the school leader, this model can produce both collaboration and conflict. To foster collaboration and avoid conflict, school leaders must be adept at managing the politics of *shared influence*. One of the most likely sources for conflict is the issue of *academic freedom*.

Academic Freedom versus Accountability

Those who advocate for academic freedom argue that teachers should control their curricular content and instructional delivery. Similar to the issue of tenure, the idea of academic freedom has its roots, and most of its application, in the college and university context. Historically, it allowed college professors to maintain complete control over instructional content and allowed for the free expression of controversial ideas. Over the years, arguments over academic freedom have migrated to the K-12 system, ultimately leading to conflict between teachers and school leaders.

Unlike other professions, teachers have, historically, been trained to work largely in isolation. This isolation is not without its benefits. Teachers enjoy considerable independence and, like their college counterparts, largely control their curricular content and instructional delivery with minimal accountability. School leaders evaluate teachers in their classrooms a few times during the year and teachers periodically submit instructional documents for administrative review. Once teachers achieve tenure, however, accountability diminishes.

Veteran educators will freely admit that their profession has changed dramatically over the last several years. Recent school reform initiatives and research on *best practices* in schools have changed the conversation about teaching and learning. Today, there is an emphasis on moving away from the old hierarchical model to one of collaboration, collegiality, and shared leadership. Leaders and teachers are beginning to tap into each other's strengths to bring the best ideas forward.

As educators in this country and around the world continue to examine school performance data, change is inevitable. As a result, teacher control over curriculum content, assessment, and instruction will likely continue to erode. As shown in figure 4.1, the emergence of the *Common Core State Standards*, *high-stakes testing*, *value-added evaluations*, and *professional learning community* organizational models are impacting and even redefining the meaning of academic freedom. More importantly, the new definition of academic freedom is signaling that the era of the independent educator is over.

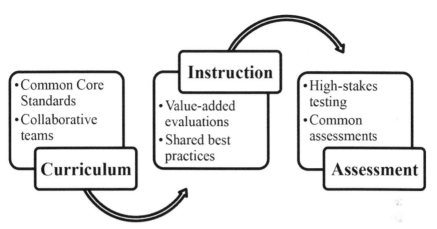

Figure 4.1 A new definition of academic freedom.

Collaboration versus Control

Enlightened leaders have realized that creating *cultures of collaboration* holds the key to authentic school improvement. In doing so, the leader disrupts long-standing practices and the status quo. Teachers will undoubtedly view this disruption as a *loss of control*. The artful leader strives to help the teacher understand that this is not the case. On the contrary, by using the collaborative model, a *culture shift* can be fostered whereby teachers gain more control over the process and use data to inform decisions about change.

In the new *collaborative model*, teachers are accountable to each other. Collaborative teaching teams determine the content of curriculum, identify best instructional practices, and craft authentic assessments together. Teams are encouraged to innovate within a common set of goals established by them. This collaborative model represents a new partnership between teachers and leaders. Under this model, challenging the status quo is encouraged as a catalyst to change and innovation. Faculty and staff are being reorganized into *professional learning communities*, and organizational charts are being flattened.

Enlightened school leaders are also embracing the collaborative model for their school leadership teams. Leaders are expected to engage in collaborative conversations with teachers about curriculum, assessment, and instruction, while staying current in the latest research on instructional leadership. Shared leadership models are rapidly becoming the norm as the old command and control, boss-subordinate models fade away.

While politics certainly existed under the command and control model, traditional boss-subordinate relationships often muted its effect. Organizational flow charts clearly indicated who was in charge and who was not. Interaction was much less collaborative and more predetermined by position. Speaking *truth to power* (authority) was infrequent. Today, under the new model, the wise leader recognizes that the strongest levels of commitment flow to the smallest part of the school organization because it is where the people's level of engagement is the highest (Dufour, Dufour, Eaker, and Many, 2010).

As schools become increasingly collaborative, interactions between professionals will increase and intensify, as will the politics. Teachers will usually agree that frequent collaboration, shared accountability, and increased collegiality among educators are welcome changes. As the era of the independent educator comes to an end, the interests of the professional learning team will come before that of the individual teacher. However, as figure 4.2 illustrates, individuals on these collaborative teams may seek to influence and control the collaborative process, placing them in conflict with the interests of the team.

The effective school leader must be fully prepared to explain the true meaning of academic freedom in the context of current education reform. The leader must foster an understanding that, while teachers tend to work largely in isolation in their own classroom, collaboration must become the new paradigm. The leader will need to make every effort to replace a culture of *compliance* with one of *commitment*. These conversations can challenge the skill set of school leaders and will require honesty, candor, courage, and trust by both leaders and teachers.

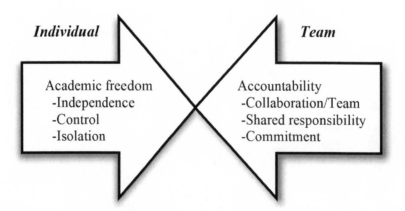

Figure 4.2   Conflict and collaboration.

The Politics of Scheduling

Few aspects of the school operation affect the quality of teaching and learning more than the master schedule. The master schedule establishes teaching assignments including grade level, subject, and content. In most schools, scheduling is a leadership decision. While it is valuable to gather input from department chairs, team leaders, and others in formal and informal leadership roles, the decision ultimately is the responsibility of the school leader (typically the principal). There are, however, cultural and political aspects of the scheduling process.

Scheduling is typically determined by three factors. The first is *logistics*. Can the schedule be built with existing space and budgetary resources while meeting contractual requirements for class size? Usually, and for budgetary reasons, the district leadership will always seek to minimize the number of full-time teachers, usually referred to as *full-time equivalents* (FTEs).

The second factor is *qualifications and credentials* of teachers. The goal is to provide a sufficient number of fully qualified teachers to teach the courses and curriculum. This ensures that teachers are qualified and competent in their content or grade level. Collective bargaining agreements often determine maximum class size. Any additional teaching assignments outside of the contractual guidelines can result in costly overloads.

The third factor, often ignored, is the *process* for determining the best teachers for classes, curriculum, and students. Is a teacher best suited for a grade level or course content? Are the strongest teachers assigned to teach courses where students struggle the most? Or, are teaching assignments determined by seniority or years of teacher service? The leader must ensure that decisions regarding teaching assignments are made with the goal in mind of optimizing student achievement.

The effective school leader must have a strong command of the data and research regarding best practices for scheduling. This information is useful when making an argument to district leadership and the board of education for reduced class size and ensuring that only highly qualified teachers are hired. The same data and research can also be useful in negotiating future collective bargaining agreements that optimize the leader's ability to assign teachers in a manner that best serves the needs of students.

The effective leader can minimize the politics of scheduling by first ensuring the school is truly *student centered*. The school leader must ensure that student success, not the convenience and demands of adults, drives scheduling decisions. This process can be difficult and is likely to be challenged by teachers. In addition, the leader must ensure an open and transparent process that involves teachers in the scheduling process.

The assignment of teachers is one of the school leader's most important decisions. For example, if a school leader assigns a class of difficult students to a teacher who struggles with classroom management, there will likely be a spike in discipline referrals. Another example is assigning a first-year teacher to an advanced placement class, resulting in the teacher being overwhelmed and possibly less than effective.

The informed school leader understands current research on best practices and that effective classroom instruction makes the greatest impact on student achievement. Armed with this research, answers to several questions can provide leaders with a useful *culture audit* regarding the assignment of teachers. Some questions that leaders need to ask include:

- Do veteran teachers receive first choice of teaching assignments?
- Are nontenured teachers asked what they want to teach?
- Are teachers regularly rotated among honors, advanced, and regular classes?
- Are the strongest teachers ever assigned classes with weaker students?
- Are honors or advanced classes assigned only to veteran teachers?
- How are teachers assigned to diverse learners or students with special needs?

The answers to these questions will provide the leader with valuable insights into the culture and politics of the school as well as the forces that shape decisions about teaching and learning.

The Politics of Relationships

The relationship between school leaders and teachers is critical to the success of students and improvement of the school. The most effective school leaders cultivate strong relationships with their faculty and staff. These relationships are often deeply rooted in trust, honesty, and respect.

Effective leaders use professional interactions, school events, and staff social events to build relationships. It is important to maintain boundaries, however, between personal and professional relationships. School leaders serve in plain view of staff and the public and must be aware that their words and actions are under scrutiny at all times. The effective school leader understands and recognizes the need for prudence and good judgment.

Most principals probably would admit that they rely on a few teachers for sage advice and good counsel. However, the savvy leader recognizes that teachers take note when leaders consistently consult with only a select few, and accusations of favoritism may emerge. The leader can prevent an unwanted, negative effect by being thoughtful and prudent when having these conversations.

POLITICS AND THE NONCERTIFIED STAFF

Amidst the ongoing discussion of teaching and learning, a group often neglected in the school organization is the noncertified staff. These employees are typically referred to as *support staff* and they include, but are not exclusive to, secretaries, administrative assistants, paraprofessionals, maintenance, custodians, groundskeepers, and other employees who do not hold a professional certification or license.

Although critical to the school mission, the debate about curriculum, assessment, and instructional practice typically does not include members of the support staff. While there are practical reasons for this, it is important to communicate the school mission, with its general academic goals, to support staff so that they can understand and support it. Failure to do so can potentially foster toxic politics among the support staff group and hinder school improvement efforts.

The wise school leader recognizes that for every professional activity performed by a teacher, there is likely a crucial activity performed by a support staff. Parent contact, word processing, printing, sorting, data management, along with building maintenance and repairs are all activities that support instruction. While not necessarily directly related to instruction, these activities all contribute to teacher effectiveness because they free teachers from these tasks and allow them to concentrate their energies on teaching and learning.

The effective school leader recognizes that a unique political dynamic exists with support staff and understands the need to optimize the relationship. Successful navigation of this dynamic is an often-neglected aspect of the school improvement process. The politics of the leader-support staff relationship is underpinned by factors that form the support staff cultural belief set. These beliefs include the support staff's perception of their role in the organization, how their work contributes to the collective work of the staff as a whole, and the extent to which their work is valued. This perception, true or not, will affect their level of commitment to the school and its leader. Table 4.1 illustrates these beliefs and the reasons why they are formed.

Negative politics within the leader-support staff relationship can be minimized if the school leader understands how to cultivate that relationship. For example, the effective school leader recognizes that those who manage the building and grounds are critical to the positive climate of the school. If the physical facility is in disrepair, or if support staff encounter ongoing difficulty

Table 4.1   Support staff beliefs

What support staff believe	Why they believe it
Feel unappreciated	Not celebrated to students and teachers
Lack understanding of vision	Mission not shared individually or as a team
Lack clarity of purpose	Told what to do but not why it is necessary
Lack understanding of their role in supporting learning	See little connection between their work, teaching, and learning
Given low priority in budgeting	See teachers consistently given first priority
Underrepresented by union	In wall-to-wall union, teachers come first
Understaffed and underresourced	Often asked to do more with less

in obtaining needed repairs and services, they will quickly become cynical about the mission of the school. Support staff that experience the leader's inability to manage the building and grounds diminish their faith in the leader in general.

Secretarial support activities must function at maximum efficiency especially in a data-driven school. The wise leader strives to provide current technology, training, and professional development for support staff. Providing professional development in technology, creating efficient work processes, and offering extra support during peak periods in the year will all contribute to a healthy culture among the support staff.

Regardless of the number of times the leader says thank you, or offers some trinket of reward on Secretaries' Day, nothing will have a more positive impact than creating a culture where support staff feel involved and empowered in their own work and the overall school improvement process. Soliciting opinions from support staff regarding their thoughts on problems and issues, especially those that directly affect their work, is key. Solutions emerging from the conversations can often surprise even the seasoned leader.

It is not uncommon for support staff to feel unappreciated. The effective leader recognizes the importance of support staff and ensures that work is valued and appreciated, and that their needs are considered. Support staff should be recognized and celebrated in front of the teachers and the students they serve. In doing so, the leaders reinforce the organizational belief that the support staff is an important part of the school mission and process. Also, the thoughtful leader who takes the time to offer a personal, heartfelt thank you for a job well done will discover that such gestures will quickly ripple through the entire support staff and improve the overall climate among the group.

The effective leader must recognize that support staff often has the first contact with parents and community. They answer telephone calls, greet parents and community members when they enter the building, and register new students when they enroll. Doing so requires a strong set of communication and public relation skills. The leader should provide professional development to enhance those skills. In addition, the leader must be ready to defend and support the support staff whenever the situation warrants.

Members of the support staff typically work closely with individual school leaders, and they will often complain that some are held more accountable than others. This requires that the building leader ensure that members of the leadership team hold each support staff member equally accountable. Leaders who rely solely on the individual work ethic of support staff will learn that what is not monitored will soon become optional.

As it becomes apparent to support staff with a strong work ethic that only some are held accountable, there will be a slow but steady decline of efficiency and effectiveness throughout the group. The politics of the leader-support staff relationship will also quickly deteriorate if individual members of the support staff are inconsistently held accountable.

The politics of the leader-support staff relationship does not have to be negative. Like teachers, support staff members seek some degree of control over their own work processes. They want to feel valued and experience a sense of reward in their work. The effective school leader recognizes this and underscores to each member of the support staff that they labor on behalf of children, that their work is important, and that their opinions matter. By doing so, the leader can integrate and enhance the work of certified and noncertified staff toward school improvement.

POLITICS AND THE SCHOOL LEADERSHIP TEAM

To this point, the focus has been on the politics of the relationship between the school leader and certified and noncertified staff. This type of "leader-to-subordinate" politics requires a distinct set of skills. The politics of the "leader-to-leader" relationship requires yet another skill set. The school leader can manage much of the former. Within the leadership team, however, the focus of the leader is to eliminate rather than simply manage the politics of the team.

Depending on the size and administrative structure of the school, the building leadership team can consist of a principal, assistant principal(s), directors, and perhaps a dean(s) who manages student behavior. In addition, schools use coordinators in a variety of departments such as technology, special education, and English Language Learner (ELL) education. Every school is unique, but elementary school teams tend to be smaller while high school teams are typically larger.

Like any collaborative relationship within the organization, members of the school leadership team may attempt to impact the political relationship of the team. They may seek to exercise control and influence the decision-making process. The wise leader understands that this dynamic can be potentially negative if left unchecked. However, if leveraged correctly, it can also be a valuable tool. The free flow of ideas and opinions is essential to creating innovative, high-performance school leadership teams. The freedom of members to challenge the team and the leader can help prevent *groupthink* and ultimately bad decisions (Hamilton, 2015).

It is a fundamental responsibility of the school leader to establish norms of behavior for all members of the leadership team. The extent to which politics corrupts the school leadership team depends on the effectiveness of the team leader. Figure 4.3 offers key rules for school leaders that will ensure a largely *apolitical* team and focus the team's energy on accomplishing the mission and vision of the school.

Rule 1: Know Your Team

Effective leaders make every effort to know their team members as professional colleagues and as individuals. Knowing the team members also requires the leader to understand who they are, their credentials, experience, and leadership philosophy. This is important especially as it pertains to their assigned position on the team. Leaders who truly know their teams can identify the strengths and challenges of each member of the team.

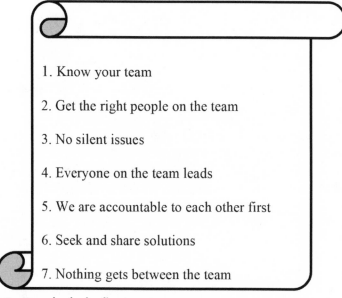

1. Know your team

2. Get the right people on the team

3. No silent issues

4. Everyone on the team leads

5. We are accountable to each other first

6. Seek and share solutions

7. Nothing gets between the team

Figure 4.3   Key rules for leading teams.

For example: What does the dean believe about student discipline and changing student behavior? What is the level of expertise and experience of the curriculum director regarding teaching and learning? Does your leadership team view the teacher evaluation process as an accountability tool or as part of professional development and growth process? Does the special education director have any affinity for the regular education environment? Is the athletic director capable of holding coaches and athletes accountable?

More often than not, new leaders will not choose their own school leadership team. Rather, they will inherit a team from the former leader. Knowing as much as possible about the former school leader and understanding the culture and politics of the team under that leader will be essential to understanding the current team. In addition, the leader should maintain a keen awareness of the team's relationship to the faculty and staff as a whole. Are leadership team members trusted and respected? Are they feared? What is the team's history and relationship with the union?

Team members bring strengths and weaknesses to the team along with their own unique personalities. Consequently, the relationship among team members is not without problems. Both challenges and close contact throughout the year are bound to create conflict. Wise school leaders know that the best teams leverage the talents and strengths of each of their individual members. They know that one team member's strengths can support another's weakness. They know that high-performing teams have a strong commitment to the work of the team.

Rule 2: Get the Right People on Your Team

Politics is not necessarily organic to a school leadership team. Whether it is to seek greater influence or increased control, it is simply a by-product of individual personality. People create the politics of the team. The savvy school leader recognizes that great leaders build teams that minimize politics. If the leader inherits the team and cannot change its composition, then every effort must be made to develop the leadership skills of each team member. If changes are to be made, the school leader must develop a screening process that will recruit individuals who are willing to accept and abide by the core values agreed on by the team. Getting the right people on the team from the beginning is the best way to prevent a toxic political environment within the team.

Rule 3: No Silent Issues

The effective leader understands that *silent issues* can quickly corrupt a team. Silent issues are concerns, problems, and even complaints among team members that, for whatever reason, go unresolved often for long periods of time. Perhaps a team member holds a grudge or lacks trust of other members of the team due to prior experience. Perhaps there is an ongoing clash of personalities. Whatever the reason, the leader must declare that silent issues have no place on the team.

Also, the leader must insist that when issues do emerge, each team member have the courage to confront each other to resolve the issue. Often team members with issues or concerns may look to the leader to intervene. While this may be appropriate in some cases, it is important for the team member to have a *critical conversation* with the colleague to get the issue resolved. As difficult as this may be, especially for less experienced leaders, these conversations will usually strengthen team relationships in the long run.

Rule 4: Everyone on the Team Leads

High-performance teams embrace a shared leadership model. Leadership positions are often formally defined by title. There may be an assistant principal for curriculum and instruction, an assistant principal for student services, a director of special education, a dean of students, or perhaps a director of building and grounds. Each of these individuals has a specific area of responsibility for which they are directly accountable. Each may view their responsibilities in slightly different ways.

Regardless of team members' understanding of their own specific responsibilities, the wise school leader understands that each member of the team must be empowered to lead. Team members will feel comfortable doing so when they believe that they have the support of the building leader. By first establishing a climate of empowerment and trust, the school leader must declare that members of the team are expected to *lead from the front*, to take ownership of the broader mission of the school team, even if it is outside their direct responsibility. The effective leader uses this shared leadership model to *connect and bond* team members. Done wisely and thoughtfully, this bond will effectively minimize or even eliminate the politics that corrupts most teams.

Rule 5: We Are Accountable to Each Other First

Everybody has a boss. Teachers report to department chairs and team leaders. The assistant principal reports to the principal. The principal reports to the superintendent, and the superintendent reports to the board of education. There is typically an organizational chart that clearly spells out who reports to whom. The school and district as a whole, of course, is accountable to the people who pay their way, the taxpayers. Within each school building, the building leadership team looks to the school leader, often the principal, as the boss.

This chain of command serves the organization well for the purposes of process and operation. However, members of a high-performance school leadership team must realize that they must be accountable to each other first. Simply put, each team member must believe that if one member of the team fails to do his or her job, all others members of the team suffer. Each has a responsibility to one another and to the team as a whole. A former high school principal shared a story that illustrates this idea:

> "Our high school had hundreds of events throughout the year, many of which required administrative supervision. I empowered my team to pick and choose those activities to supervise. I always made sure I chose a few more than any of my team because I felt it was my responsibility as principal to do so. Some, like football games, required all of us to be there and those were long nights for all; often cold and it seemed like it was always raining. The superintendent required an administrator to remain after the games until all students left school grounds, making the night even longer. As a team, we didn't like it, but the superintendent made it clear what he expected us to do.
>
> To reduce the load for all, we established a rotation using teams of two who would remain after the games until all students were gone. It worked well. But I remember joking with my team that I was glad the rotation allowed some to leave after the games but, if while driving away, they didn't feel just a little bit guilty leaving their colleagues standing in the rain, then I'd worry a bit about their commitment to the team. We laughed about it but we all knew what it meant. And, I think that on those nights when all but two were able to leave, the rest did feel just a little bit guilty. I know I did." (Anonymous, 2015)

When team members hold each other accountable, negative and corruptive politics cannot survive. By establishing and nurturing a team climate of *mutual accountability*, the school leader can optimize the talents of every member of the team.

Rule 6: Seek and Share Solutions

One thing is certain. Politics is just one of the problems faced by today's school leaders. Every day of the school year brings new problems, even if existing ones have yet to be fully resolved. The skilled school leader accepts this as simply part of the job and treats these problems as mere challenges to be overcome.

With this in mind, the skilled leader also recognizes that to strengthen the team and minimize corruptive politics, members of the team are expected to be *solution generators* even if it is outside their area of direct responsibility.

One principal referred to this process as *pushing the conversation* or requiring that each member of the team be willing to challenge the status quo by asking "why, why not, who says, why can't we, and what if?"

For example, Toyota leaders, managers, engineers, and designers are trained to ask the *five whys*. When approaching a problem, they will ask "why?" five times to reach the root cause, not just the symptom, of the problem (Five Whys, 2015). Great teams support and challenge each other to find solutions.

Rule 7: Nothing Gets Between the Team

Nothing gets between the team, not problems, silent issues, job descriptions, personalities, or politics. Members of the school leadership team typically report to the principal. Wise principals understand that to be effective leaders and eliminate politics within the team, team members must be treated as coequals. They know that the leader is *first among equals* as opposed to being the "boss." High-performing teams of committed professionals know their responsibilities. Wise school leaders should declare that the only thing the leader owns exclusively is the ultimate responsibility, that the team shares everything else.

Effective school leaders assure their team members that they will be supported when faced with criticism. Team members will know that they can recover from a mistake and that, while they might suffer the leader's criticism privately, they will never suffer it publicly. A highly effective leader drives out fear and creates a bond that will unite team members and sustain them in times of challenge and difficulty.

Politics can be the mortal enemy of teams. School leaders who know and understand this strive to remove politics from the team by empowering and supporting the team. They drive decision-making down to team members. They foster a climate of support that is free of fear. They constantly reinforce the idea that every member of the team is accountable to each other first. The effective school leader will check members of the team who violate the norm or who place their own interests and agenda ahead of the team. When used effectively, the concept of "nothing gets between the team" can be a powerful force for creating high-performance school leadership teams.

Lead, Manage, Facilitate

Effective leaders who know when to lead, when to manage, and when to facilitate can affect the dynamic within the school. Competent leaders also know that these three roles are interrelated and are appropriate in specific situations (see figure 4.4).

Figure 4.4 The three roles of leaders.

Setting and reinforcing the vision demands strong leadership. Building operation, facilities, and logistics demand effective, competent management skills. Using professional development to foster a culture of collaboration that empowers faculty and staff will demand effective facilitator skills. Effective leaders will use a combination of these skill sets to move the school organization forward.

Optics and Perception

The skilled school leader understands that *optics* play an important role in school politics. Optics refers to the way things appear, the perception of the leader, and, more often than not, the state of the school. The leader who disregards how things are perceived fails to follow the old political adage that *perception is reality*.

For example, faculty, staff, and even students may perceive that student behavior in the school building is deteriorating, even out of control. Discipline data indicate, however, that the vast majority of student discipline involves minor offenses. The unskilled leader dismisses these perceptions as mere grumbling by uninformed or malcontent faculty and staff. The skilled school leader recognizes the importance of optics in this situation and moves quickly to educate the faculty and staff regarding the facts. The leader may even provide a regular *state of the school* report to faculty and staff throughout the year that can include, among other things, facts about student discipline.

Words Matter

Leaders govern with words. The leadership style and the politics of the school organization are connected by the spoken and written words of its leaders. The skilled school leader understands and strives to become an effective *wordsmith* recognizing that what is said, and how it is said, can make all the difference. The wording of formal correspondence, presentations to staff, casual comments to teachers, and even assembly presentations to students can influence school politics.

Words are remembered. Individuals and groups memorialize words. More than one school leader has been held accountable for the spoken or written word left only to remark, "That's not what I meant." Effective school leaders choose their words carefully. They say what they mean and mean what they say. They also recognize that words influence action. If positive action for change and improvement is the goal, then the use of influential and inspiring words, reinforced by bold action, will be essential to success.

Actions Matter More

Words matter and actions matter even more. Ralph Waldo Emerson cautioned, "What you do speaks so loudly that I cannot hear what you say" (Emerson, 2010). Leaders who consistently say one thing and do another will soon lose their credibility. If they do it enough, they'll also lose their job. Effective school leaders seize every opportunity to reinforce their vision and take action that reflects their words.

Leaders who say they support teachers must demonstrate that support when the unreasonable or difficult parent confronts a teacher. In a truly student-centered school, decisions are made with students, not adults, as the priority. Similarly, leaders who ask for honesty and candor from faculty and staff must be willing to hear it when it's offered.

Talk Less, Listen More

There are people who listen and people who wait to talk. Becoming an effective listener can greatly enhance the leader's relationship with faculty and staff and have a very positive effect on the political relationships within the school. Leaders who make time to listen will quickly garner support and respect throughout the school building. Truly great school leaders frequently self-assess their leadership skills and seek to continuously improve. At the same time, they remain keen observers of the politics within their school.

Leaders, like most people, can't fundamentally change who they are. But they can change how they act, be thoughtful about what they say and write, and strive to be better listeners. Great leaders recognize their short-comings, and strive to improve them. They craft a personal leadership style that is open and honest, but they also know that style without substance is no leadership at all.

SUMMARY

School leaders are faced with a multitude of challenges as they attempt to adapt and adjust to the current wave of educational change and reform. Command and control models are fading away, and the era of the independent educator is coming to an end. Teachers, support staff, and the school leadership team should reexamine their roles and relationships as the new collaborative, collegial models emerge. Those who aspire to become transformational leaders will need strong interpersonal skills in order to influence those who do the work of school reform. Understanding the *politics of influence* and interaction with faculty, staff, and leaders will be critical to the leader's success.

Effective school leaders should be mindful of the importance of style, words, and action as they seek to influence the people and the process. Paying close attention to the optics of the work while recognizing that perception is reality can minimize the negative, corrosive politics that often permeate the school dynamic. School leaders who seek to have a transformational impact on student achievement also recognize that the manner in which schedules are designed is critical. Adjusting teacher assignments to optimize student success will invariably disrupt the status quo and challenge the leader to navigate difficult conversations with teachers. The transformational school leader will make decisions with students, not adults, as the first priority.

As the school reform movement gains momentum, schools and their leaders will face increasing uncertainty. One thing that is certain, as long as there are parents, community members, students, leaders, teachers, and support staff in schools, there will be politics. The extent to which school leaders can create healthy school cultures and successfully navigate its politics may well make up the larger measure of their success.

CASE STUDY

You are the new principal of a large middle school, and there are several administrators on your team. Members of your team are in the early or middle years of their careers. One of them, the dean, has been at your school for 22 years and has more than 30 years of experience in public school education. He is highly respected and well thought of by faculty and staff.

When the principal position was posted, he applied for it at the same time you applied. You have since learned that many thought he would get the position as he had been at the school for most of his career. You are now the principal, and he is on your building leadership team. You view his many years of experience as a valuable asset to the school. You also recognize that he harbors some resentment because he did not get the principal position.

What challenges does this relationship dynamic present? What is your strategy for optimizing your relationship with the dean? What will you say to the dean to ensure that he will continue to contribute to the collective efforts of the school building team? Describe the specifics of your conversation with the dean.

EXERCISES AND DISCUSSION QUESTIONS

1. A core value of your team is "nothing gets between the team." One of your building team members repeatedly violates this core value by harboring hard feelings for another team member. Team meetings have become confrontational between the two members of your team. Describe your "critical conversation" with these team members. How will you facilitate a resolution of this conflict? What will you say to the team member who violated this core value?

2. In observing the actions and interactions of your team, you notice that a dean struggles with conflict resolution, especially with parents of students. Parents have complained to you, and to the superintendent, that he is very difficult. They have described him as a "bully" and demand that his behavior be addressed. Describe your efforts to determine the facts of this situation and address the behavior of the dean.

3. Due to a retirement, a leadership position in your building team has been posted. What criteria will you use to select a candidate for the position? Describe the process and characteristics that you will identify as critical to the candidate joining your team. Describe the characteristics of an ideal candidate for this position.

4. A union grievance has been filed against a member of your leadership team. The union is claiming that your team member has a gender bias and treats female teachers differently than male teachers. Privately, you have observed him using language indicating gender bias but you have no evidence that he is biased or unfair in his professional work. Aside from managing the formal grievance process, describe how you would handle this situation with your team member. What would be the key points of that conversation? Be specific.

REFERENCES

Dufour, R., Dufour, R., Eaker, R., and Many, T. (2010). *Learning by Doing: A Handbook for Professional Communities at Work. A Practical Guide for PLC Teams and Leadership.* Bloomington, Indiana: Solution Tree Press.

Emerson, R.W. (2010). *Letters and Social Aims.* Boston: Harvard University Press.

Five Whys: Getting to the root of the problem quickly. (2015). *Mind Tools.* Retrieved from http://www.mindtools.com/pages/article/newTMC_5W.htm.

Hamilton, N. (2015). *Getting the Right People in and the Wrong People out of the Firm or Department.* Retrieved from University of St. Thomas, Holloran Center Web site: http://www.stthomas.edu/media/hollorancenter/pdf/GettingtheRightPe.pdf.

Chapter 5

Who's In Charge Here?
The Politics of the Union-
Administration Relationship

OBJECTIVES

At the conclusion of this chapter you will be able to:

1. Describe the different features of unions and their overall impact on school life (ELCC 5, 6; InTASC 3, 9, 10; ISLLC 6; TLEC 1, 3, 6, 7).
2. List and describe the different union leadership positions and their roles (ELCC 6; InTASC 3, 9, 10; ISLLC 3, 6; TLEC 1, 3, 6, 7).
3. List and describe the critical factors of union-administration politics (ELCC 3; InTASC 3, 9, 10; ISLLC 3, 6; TLEC 1, 3, 6, 7).
4. Describe the impact of state and federal initiatives on union-administration politics (ELCC 6; InTASC 3, 9, 10; ISLLC 3, 6; TLEC 1, 3, 6, 7).

UNIONS AS PART OF SCHOOL LIFE

Unions are part of school life and like it or not, they are here to stay. Every school leader must be competent in engaging and collaborating with unions, its leaders, and the politics of that relationship. For the new leader, doing so can be intimidating and difficult. A variety of factors will contribute to a healthy and productive relationship between union and school leadership.

It is the responsibility of the skilled leader to embrace the relationship with the union and view that relationship as an opportunity to collaborate for school improvement and change. Doing so requires both a solid understanding of the role of the union in the school as well as steady willingness to set a high standard of integrity in all aspects of the relationship with union members and leaders.

Unions have been an integral part of American public education for more than a century. For most of the twentieth century, the *National Education Association* presented itself as an alliance of educators, a professional organization and not a traditional labor union. The *American Federation of Teachers*, founded in 1916, has always been recognized as a true union taking its place among organized labor unions formed after the Wagner Act of 1935.

During the 1960s, teacher pay slipped dramatically compared to other professional occupations. As a result, the AFT became more attractive to teachers who for many years were more comfortable belonging to a *professional association* such as the NEA. In the wake of the increasing gains achieved by organized labor in other sectors of the labor force, teachers were drawn to a union who would help them achieve gains similar to other labor unions.

By the 1980s, teacher unions made significant gains in pay and benefits. More importantly, they increasingly restricted the ability of administrations and school boards to hire, fire, and in general, hold staff accountable for their actions and performance. As a result and over time, the line between private and public sector labor-management relations became almost indistinguishable. As a result, most of those in and out of education came to view the relationship between unions and school administrations as inherently adversarial.

Teacher unions affect several aspects of school life. Selection of teachers, choice of curriculum, placement of students, and even board of education policy can be impacted by union-administration politics. The primary function of teacher unions, however, is to act as the *collective bargaining agent* for the membership. This includes the negotiating of contracts and representing individual members in labor disputes or disciplinary actions.

Those staff members who are represented by the union are referred to as the *bargaining unit*. The binding legal agreement between the union and the administration is called the *collective bargaining agreement* and commonly referred to as the *contract*.

Members and nonmembers of their respective unions pay dues to support the union efforts on their behalf. *Fair share* legislation provides that every person employed in a position covered by that bargaining unit must pay union dues that represent a fair share of the cost of services provided by the union.

When challenged on the fair share issue, unions will always argue that since all personnel of the school or district benefit from the negotiated contract, all should contribute their fair share, and that even if individual teachers and staff members choose not to join the union, they should pay a portion or even all of the union dues. State law typically determines the amount of fair share dues paid by teachers.

A few positions in the school may be considered outside the bargaining unit if the member works in a sensitive position that might compromise aspects of either the union or the administration. An example of this might be the superintendent's secretary position. While being eligible for union membership, this *position* is usually negotiated out of the bargaining unit because the position has access to confidential or sensitive material.

If the school is operating under a collectively bargained agreement, the union represents all members of that bargaining unit. In most schools, one union, either the NEA or the AFT, may also represent the noncertified staff. This is commonly known as a *wall-to-wall* union. In some schools, teachers and staff have separate unions and contracts. From the union standpoint, one contract is preferable because it offers solidarity and leverage in the event of a labor dispute and contract negotiations. District leaders often prefer a *wall-to-wall* contract as well because it requires negotiations with only one representative group.

Unfortunately, history has proven too often that wall-to-wall union leaders can focus too much energy and effort on representing certified staff (teachers) leaving noncertified staff (support) underrepresented. Whether employees choose a wall-to-wall or separate contract can depend on a variety of factors. Those factors include the history of staff-administration relations, the relationship between certified and noncertified staff, and the overall culture of the district.

FACTORS INFLUENCING UNION-ADMINISTRATION POLITICS

It is a commonly held idea that the relationship between unions and administrations in schools must be adversarial, that it must be defined by conflict. It does not have to be so. The transformational leader understands that the common ground between the union and administration is a process of give and take.

Leaders on both sides understand that achieving sustainable change and improvement must be a shared goal, and to seek that end is the true work of *transformational* leaders. A key point of understanding is that the union-administration relationship, while hopefully collegial and collaborative, is a decidedly *political* relationship and is affected by a variety of factors internal and external as shown in figure 5.1.

Many view politics as something negative, something to be avoided, the dark side of human interaction. Without question, politics is often characterized by intrigue, manipulation, and betrayal. Politics, however, does not have to be negative. Politics is, by definition, the competition among competing interest groups or individuals for power and leadership within an organization. Whether in government, business, or school organizations, politics is ultimately all about *who has the power*. In the school environment, that power

Internal Influences	External Influences
Union structure	Federal initiatives
Union leader style	State intiatives
Internal politics	Community politics
School culture and history	Employment laws
Leader attributes and actions	School board
	Public perception

Figure 5.1   Influences on union-administration politics.

can impact daily school operation, policies, and procedures, and even shape the mission, vision, and direction of the school or district.

The union seeks greater power in order to *influence* policy and decisions in the interests of its members. The administration seeks power and control in order to move the school forward and advance the interests and agenda of the school board and other stakeholders. The give and take that results from this give-and-take process *should* create what diplomats call the *art of the possible, the attainable, and the art of the next best*. In diplomatic circles, this is also referred to as realistic politics or *realpolitik*, the common ground where common agreement can be reached.

The school leader must recognize that negotiations and conflict resolution between union and administration cannot be a zero-sum, win or lose process. Agreement is more often the result of what both sides can live with. Leaders who understand that the common ground is often found through compromise are more likely to have productive dialogue and solve complex problems.

THE ROLE OF THE UNION LEADERS

Union leaders are typically elected annually by a general membership vote. The structure of union leadership is similar to many other professional organizations. Typical union leadership structure includes an executive board, a president, vice president, secretary, treasurer, grievance chair, and building representatives. The building-level leader will have more frequent contact with the building representative or the grievance chair as most elected officers of the union typically work more closely with district administration.

The Building Representative

In most schools settings, unions will usually appoint or elect a *building representative*, often referred to simply as the *building rep*, who serves as the intermediary between the staff and the principal. Members can then bring concerns, grievances, and other matters to the union representative, thus relieving an individual staff member from having to bring those issues directly to the principal. The building representative also plays an important role in representing members in disciplinary situations. In a wall-to-wall union, one that includes certified staff and noncertified staff, one rep will serve the entire staff. If noncertified staff is organized separately, they will have their own rep.

The role of the building rep is critical to the success of the union-administration relationship. While school leaders have no role in choosing the rep, the relationship with the building rep serves to help build *trust* enabling both sides to resolve issues and problems before they become more serious.

To serve this end, the school leader, typically the principal, should schedule regular meetings with the building rep throughout the year to discuss issues of concern to both parties in order to prevent any escalation of emerging issues. By scheduling regular conversations with the building rep, the school leader can build mutual trust and confidence. These meetings can also serve as a mutually beneficial *"weather report"* allowing both to comment on current school *climate* and general staff-administration relations in the building.

The school leader and the building rep should also agree to a *no surprises* rule with both parties agreeing to never allow each other to be caught off guard by a union grievance or administrative disciplinary action against a staff member. Both will agree to provide an early storm warning if a major issue is emerging. In this way, both can work toward a positive resolution before either is compelled to take formal action.

Honesty, candor, and transparency form the basic elements of the mutual commitment by both sides to honor each other's word. Any breach of this trust can have long-lasting ramifications so it is important that leaders on both sides make the commitment and honor it throughout the relationship.

The building rep can also serve as an effective mediator or go-between as conflict arises between staff and administration. When an issue arises that may lead to a grievance, the rep can facilitate conversations with leaders that can lead to a positive resolution of the problem before it rises to the level of a formal grievance.

In addition to the planned meetings and conversations, there is another kind of dialogue between the two leaders that can lead to greater understanding of shared goals. As the relationship between union and school leaders becomes stronger, opportunities for candor and frank conversation will occur often outside of the formal meeting. These conversations are referred to as *sidebar* discussions. As trust and confidence is established between union and school leaders, it will often be the sidebar discussions that lead to reducing resistance to change, solving problems, and turning ideas into action.

The enlightened school leader will also strive to make the union leader a *partner* in the overall school improvement process. Doing so is a key feature in crafting the *art of the possible* and will take time to build. Once accomplished, however, this partnership can be a powerful force for school change and improvement.

The Grievance Chair

The *grievance chair* is appointed by the union and is usually a teacher or staff member in the building. The role of the grievance chair is to represent the union member in the event that a formal grievance is filed against the administration. The principal and grievance chair typically meet when a grievance is filed or when there is reason to believe that one may be filed.

A *grievance* is an *allegation* by the union that the collective bargaining agreement or contract has been violated. An example of a typical grievance might occur when the collective bargaining agreement provides teachers with a duty-free lunch period but the principal assigns some teachers to supervision during their lunch. In this case, the union member(s) can file a formal grievance if it is not informally resolved.

The grievance process usually involves a reading of the grievance, a union demand for *remedy* or solution to the grievance, a written response by the school leader, and finally a meeting between the grievance chair and principal or designee to resolve the grievance. If the grievance is not addressed or resolved satisfactorily, it could result in further action by the union.

One important feature of the grievance is worthy of note. Often the word grievance is used to describe actions that do not meet the definition of a grievance. It is important to understand that a grievance is a formal term and speaks to a specific legal process. A grievance is defined as a *breach* or *violation* of the collective bargaining agreement (contract). Anything else is not a grievance. A *complaint* is not a grievance, and the competent union leader will advise his members as to what constitutes a grievance and what does not.

In a toxic school culture without competent union leaders, every issue may become a grievance. If the school leader and building rep have a collegial and collaborative relationship and the teachers and staff are comfortable speaking directly to the school leader, problems often can be resolved very quickly.

An example of this dynamic might involve a teacher speaking with the building rep and principal about being treated poorly by another administrator. After listening to the teacher and carefully considering the facts of the situation, the principal can then commit to resolving the issue by speaking to that administrator. The principal will then make sure to follow up with the teacher and the building rep or grievance chair regarding the resolution of the issue. In this manner, a formal grievance can be avoided.

The frequency of formal grievances can also be an indicator of the state of the school *culture*. If grievances are frequent, it is important for the leader to ask why this is occurring as deeper cultural problems may be causing general staff discontent. Frequent grievances over *minor* issues are usually considered *nuisance* grievances, as they may not meet the standard for a grievance even though they are formally submitted.

They are more often filed as a symbolic gesture toward an administration perceived as being uncooperative, unresponsive, or heavy-handed. The frequent occurrence of nuisance grievances is usually a strong indicator of a toxic school culture. This can impact the entire organization.

Whether the grievance is considered nuisance or legitimate, every grievance must be handled through the formal grievance process. Throughout the process, the grievance chair will serve as the formal representative of the union as the issue moves to resolution. The grievance process also has a *time limit* and must be completed within the guidelines stated in the collective bargaining agreement.

In a healthy school culture, most leaders and staff want to avoid grievances, as they are time-consuming, and can permanently damage relationships and negatively affect the climate of the school. Enlightened leaders know that grievances represent a breakdown among colleagues and should not to be taken lightly by either union or administration.

Union Leader Style: Delegate or Trustee?

Union leaders often can be characterized by two distinct leadership styles. The effective school leader who can recognize these styles will be better equipped to manage the politics of the relationship with the union. Also, understanding the style and personality of union leaders will allow school leaders to adjust their own style in the hope of fostering a more collegial school climate.

The first union leadership style is called the *delegate* style. These union leaders see themselves as representatives or *delegates* chosen by the members and tasked first and foremost with advancing the specific interests of the membership regardless of their own personal position on the issue.

If the members want union leaders to pursue a particular course of action in negotiations or with individual members, delegate-style union leaders will follow the direction of the membership regardless of their own individual position on the issue. If the school culture is healthy, delegate-style leaders will frequently collaborate with school leaders and conflict usually will be minimal.

The second union leadership style is that of a *trustee*. Trustee-style leaders see themselves as elected or appointed representatives of the members but feel that they are *empowered* to act with the greater good in mind, that they seek to act in the best interest of most members or even serve the best interest of the school as a whole.

The trustee style can be effective if the union leader has a strong understanding of the role of the union and believes in the mission and vision of the school. Unfortunately, however, more narcissistic and self-interested union leaders also seem to be drawn to the trustee style, and if this occurs, they may elect to place their own interests ahead of that of the general membership.

For example, if a policy change increases the teaching load of that particular union leader or perhaps threatens the jobs of personal friends, some trustee-style leaders may place personal gain before professional responsibility. Left unchecked over time, this abuse of power can contribute to the development of an *adult-centered* school culture rather than one that is *student centered.*

One deviation from both these styles of leadership is the union leader who is not popular with the membership but manages to lead through intimidation and fear. These individuals are sometimes referred to as *combative*-style union leaders. While less common and often the result of an already toxic culture, this style of union leadership can present unique challenges for the school leader.

Combative-style union leaders usually retain their leadership position largely as a result of an already existing adversarial climate between staff and administration. These combative-style leaders are unafraid to challenge and disrupt administration initiatives and are often seen by their members as willing to do what no one else will. The combative union leader can become a distraction, will test the patience of an administration, and will certainly challenge school leaders to maintain their professionalism and avoid confrontation.

Regardless of the style of both groups of leaders, trust *must* always anchor the union-administration relationship. Trust is a fragile commodity that should be valued and protected. Leaders must always honor their word and their promises, and they must always follow through. Experienced leaders recognize that it takes much longer to establish trust with the union than it does to destroy it.

The leader must also strive to maintain a high level of professionalism at all times. One example of this is the leader's need to avoid conversations with teachers and staff that might reveal confidential information between union and school leaders. While leaders may be tempted to do so in order to ingratiate themselves with a particular staff member, doing so can permanently damage the union-administration relationship.

If tempted to share information, smart leaders know that everyone has one confidant, one person with whom they share everything . . . *everything*. More than one administrative career has come to an end as a result of a poorly chosen conversation or email. If you want information to remain confidential, don't say anything to anyone!

THE PARADOX OF THE UNION-ADMINISTRATION RELATIONSHIP

Having discussed the role of the union leaders, it is useful to point out that a paradox exists within the union-administration political dynamic. This paradox can often be disheartening especially to the new leader, who often finds it difficult to understand why there is strong union resistance to a change initiative that everyone in the school organization agrees is a good idea.

As stated earlier in this chapter, the core purpose of the union is to represent the interests of its members, to advocate on their behalf. The school leader must then recognize that *any* change initiative is likely to meet resistance from the union even if the law or district policy mandates the initiative or it is clearly recognized by all to be beneficial to the school. This paradox occurs because union leaders are predisposed to challenge any change to the status quo as potentially harmful to the members. While the union may not be able to ultimately block the change, they likely will challenge it when proposed and possibly even delay or disrupt its implementation.

School leaders who face these challenges with a positive, collaborative spirit, it will foster meaningful dialogue between union and administrators, which, in turn, will lead to a shared commitment to move forward. Maintaining open, honest dialogue can test the skill set of the school leader, and while there are many leadership traits that are essential, six attributes emerge as being critical to building positive union-administration relationships (see figure 5.2).

The first critical attribute for establishing and sustaining a positive political relationship with the union is the leader's ability to build a *reservoir of trust*

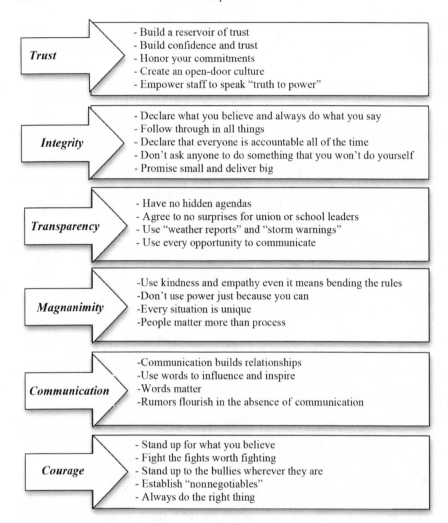

Figure 5.2   Key attributes and actions for leaders.

with staff that will lead to finding common ground on important issues. The concept of the reservoir of trust is rooted in the belief that if a leader accepts a challenge, takes reasonable and deliberate steps to accomplish positive change, and believes that those who disagree are honorable and well intended, the process will ultimately yield results and lead all to common ground.

The first challenge for the new leader is to begin to build a reservoir of trust with all teachers, staff, *and* their union leaders through word and action. The words and actions of the leader, especially the new leader, will be closely watched particularly in the early months. Leaders should seek every opportunity to demonstrate to the union, staff, and students that they stand behind what they say and can be trusted that the words of the leader will be supported by ethical action.

The second attribute is *integrity*. Integrity must be a core value for any leader. School leaders should be prepared to declare what they believe, use every opportunity to reinforce the message of those beliefs, and demonstrate a *bias for action* regarding those beliefs. Staff members expect leaders to follow through on commitments and promises. However, leaders should also be careful not to promise what they may not be able to deliver. The mayor of New York, Rudy Giuliani, frequently advised his staff to always "promise small and deliver big" (Giuliani, 2002).

Most of all, school leaders with integrity are true to their word and never duplicitous in their words and actions. They are ever conscious that leaders govern with words and those words will be remembered. Nothing will fuel union animosity faster than the perception that the school leader says only what best serves his or her own interests.

The third attribute that will contribute to positive union-administration politics is *transparency*. While the word may be a bit overused, it is a widely accepted idea that hidden agendas and a lack of transparency can be professionally fatal to a school leader as well as destructive to the school climate.

An example of the need for transparency often arises during decisions about budget and especially staffing. For example, if staff reductions are likely as result of budget cuts, it is important for the union to know as early as possible to allow them to manage concerns and conversations with their members. It is a mistake to conceal this information because if the union learns that their confidence has been violated, it will significantly breach the union's trust of the administration.

In today's climate of scandal and abuse of power, there is heightened scrutiny of leadership at every level. While the leader may not be allowed to share certain sensitive information, wherever possible, the union should be kept informed of developments that might affect their members. There should be no hidden agendas and the storm warning/weather report commitment should be always honored.

The fourth attribute is *magnanimity*. While not often discussed in school leadership texts, being magnanimous is an artful leadership trait that can be used to develop and enhance union and staff relations. Magnanimity demands a generous and empathetic approach to school leadership. It calls upon the school leader to sometimes look beyond the rules and policies and consider the human element involved in the collective work of the school.

Magnanimity often is needed when considering disciplinary action involving a staff member or when a staff member is going through a personal crisis that is impacting his or her work in some way. In this situation, the leader may have to weigh the specific aspects of the situation against the need to enforce the rule. While it may not be easy, giving that staff member some consideration will lead the staff and the union to recognize that that they work for an empathetic leader who understands the need to work *with* people and that people come before policy.

It might be useful to say a word here about consistency. Often what will prevent the school leader from being magnanimous or making exceptions to policy is the fear of appearing inconsistent. Consistency is certainly an admirable leadership trait, and clearly, being consistent in word and practice is important to demonstrate integrity. However, many school leaders will admit that in their role, there are sufficient opportunities to demonstrate consistency but far fewer opportunities to demonstrate the *human* side of leadership. Confident school leaders know that they can be fair and empathetic without being weak.

The effective school leader recognizes that every situation is unique and should be considered on its own merit. This situation often arises when dealing with staff requests for sick and personal leave days. The individual situation should dictate the leader's action, and courageous leaders should not always sacrifice those opportunities for the sake of consistency. Striking a good balance between consistency and magnanimity will result in both staff and union seeing the leader as authentic, confident, and courageous.

The fifth critical attribute is *communication*. Union leaders and staff will most often criticize school leaders because of their failure to communicate sufficiently and effectively. Current communication technology affords leaders ample opportunity to communicate with staff, parents, and students. To maintain a strong relationship with the union, school leaders should seize every opportunity to do so. Communication also includes the need for the leader to be *visible* throughout the building. Effective leaders know that visibility is simply one more form of communication that will increase *accessibility* and enhance communication and trust.

The sixth and final attribute contributing to positive union-administration politics is *courage*. Courage demands that leaders be willing to stand up for what they believe, to fight the fights worth fighting. Teachers need courageous leaders who will defend them against an unreasonable parent or disgruntled member of the community. The courageous leader must be prepared to resist unreasonable union demands and may even need to stand up to a superior on behalf of a teacher or student.

Most leaders will come to define courage in their own way usually through a combination of education and experience. History, literature, and politics certainly offer many examples of courageous leadership, and school leaders can draw wisdom from their own personal experiences as well. School leaders should look to those examples of courage and strive to emulate those key attributes of leader actions as shown in figure 5.2.

Effective leaders understand that some things are nonnegotiable, that some things really are either right or wrong. While leaders can't make every issue a battle, they must recognize that some things are worth fighting for. John F. Kennedy offered his own advice to any leader who faces a crisis of conscience:

> These, then, are some of the pressures which confront a man of conscience. He cannot ignore the pressure groups, his constituents, his party, the comradeship of his colleagues, the needs of his family, his own pride in office, the necessity for compromise and the importance of remaining in office. He must judge for himself which path to choose, which step will most help or hinder the ideals to which he is committed. He realizes that once he begins to weigh each issue in terms of his chances for reelection, once he begins to compromise away his principles on one issue or another for fear that to do otherwise would halt his career and prevent future fights for principle, then he has lost the very freedom of conscience which justifies his continuance in office. But to decide at which point and on which issue he will risk his career is a difficult and soul-searching decision. (John F. Kennedy, written during his time as Senator in 1955)

THE POLITICS OF FEDERAL AND STATE INITIATIVES

Since the passage of the ESEA and the release of *A Nation at Risk* in 1983, the conversation regarding school improvement has been driven by data indicating that American students were falling behind the rest of the world and becoming increasingly less competitive in the global marketplace.

Over the last thirty years, five major reform initiatives profoundly affected American education and began to alter the politics of unions and administrations across the country. The debate over testing, best teaching practices, teacher quality, accountability in schools, the role of teacher unions, and the priorities of American schools began to change beginning in 1983 as shown in figure 5.3.

In 1983, The National Commission on Excellence in Education, appointed by Education Secretary Terrell Bell, issued a report entitled *A Nation at Risk*. This report was the result of an eighteen-month study, concentrated primarily on secondary education, and found that the curriculum in American high schools as a whole no longer had a central purpose unifying all of the subjects.

The report found that American education was underperforming and what was unimaginable a generation ago had begun to occur: that other nations were matching and surpassing our educational performance. One finding of

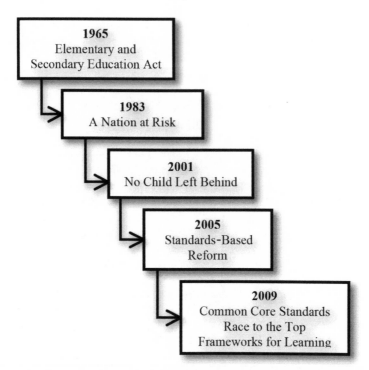

Figure 5.3   Reforms affecting union-administration relations.

this report showed that twenty-three million American adults were functionally illiterate by the simplest test of everyday reading, writing, and com-
prehension. The report also showed that about 13 percent of all American
seventeen-year-olds could be considered functionally illiterate.

The report went on to say that the poor state of American education also
could have economic repercussions. It warned that as long as American
education continued to decline, our competitive edge in the global market
economy would also continue to decline. The findings of this report were
considered particularly depressing as the demand for highly skilled workers
in scientific and technological fields climbed to an all-time high.

As a result, the report suggested five changes to the curriculum of American high schools. Those changes included requiring four years of English,
three years of math, three years of science, three years of social studies, and
half a year of computer science. Specific standards were established as to
what should be accomplished in these five basic content areas.

The report argued that these changes would enable American students to
achieve excellence as defined by the National Commission on Excellence
in Education: "A school or college that sets high expectations and goals for

all learners and strives in every way possible to help students reach them." In addition to these changes, it was also proposed that the study of foreign languages begin in the elementary schools.

As a way to increase our educational standing in the world, the commission suggested that teaching, teacher education, and education standards also be reformed. The virtues of lifelong learning for all were also extolled. The report cited a high demand for increased support for those who teach mathematics, science, and foreign languages. The need for education specialists for gifted and talented, language minority, and handicapped students is also crucial.

In addition, the report found that those who were interested in the field of education were too often not academically qualified, that teacher preparation curriculum was weighted heavily with courses in education methods at the expense of courses in the subjects to be taught. The report also encouraged the raising of teacher salaries in order to attract and retain qualified teachers as well as the institution of merit pay and incentives such as grants and loans.

The impact of *A Nation at Risk* on unions and school leadership was dramatic. For the first time since the launch of the Soviet satellite Sputnik in 1957, educators and the general public raised serious questions about the efficacy of our educational system. Those questions quickly turned to debate about teachers and classroom practice and provoked unions to go on the defensive. *A Nation at Risk* fueled a new debate between unions and leaders regarding student performance, teacher evaluation, and accountability. In addition, educators at every level revisited the validity of curriculum, instructional practice, testing, and the elements that defined a quality school.

No Child Left Behind

Three days after taking office in January 2001 as the forty-third president of the United States, George W. Bush announced No Child Left Behind, his framework for bipartisan education reform that he described as "the cornerstone of my administration." President Bush emphasized his deep belief in our public schools, but an even greater concern that "too many of our neediest children are being left behind," despite the nearly $200 billion in federal spending since the passage of the ESEA.

The president called for bipartisan solutions based on accountability, choice, and flexibility in federal education programs. Less than a year later and despite the unprecedented challenges of engineering an economic recovery while leading the nation in the war on terrorism following the events of September 11, President Bush secured passage of the landmark NCLB Act. This new law reflected a remarkable bipartisan consensus first articulated in the president's No Child Left Behind framework on how to improve the performance of American elementary and secondary schools while at the same time ensuring that no child became trapped in a failing school.

The NCLB Act, which reauthorized the ESEA, incorporated the principles and strategies proposed by President Bush. These included increased accountability for states, school districts, and schools; greater choice for parents and students, particularly those attending low-performing schools; more flexibility for states and local educational agencies (LEAs) in the use of federal education dollars; and a stronger emphasis on reading, especially for our youngest children.

The key elements of the NCLB included:

- Increased accountability
- More choices for parents and students
- Greater flexibility for states, school districts, and schools
- Putting reading first

NCLB accelerated the education reform movement and caused national union leaders to become increasingly defensive regarding those reforms. Under constant criticism from several sectors, teacher unions and their members assumed increasing strident positions about salary and working conditions along with changes in school curriculum, assessment, and instructional practice.

At the local level, school administrations, under pressure from parents and local school boards to show improvement, increased demands on teachers to improve their professional practice and show greater student achievement. NCLB evolved as the policy outcome of the discussion triggered earlier by *A Nation at Risk*, thereby introducing a new era of accountability for teachers and the unions that led them.

Standards-Based Reform

As the national education reform movement gained steam and the demand for accountability of student outcomes grew stronger, individual states moved quickly to establish their own sets of academic and curricular standards. The result of this effort was a set of standards that varied widely from state to state. In addition, it become quickly apparent to school officials and teachers not only that these standards were complex and wordy in their descriptions, but also that the sheer number of standards made it impossible for teachers and schools to complete the curriculum objectives during the course of a student's educational career.

Common Core

For years, it had been argued that the academic progress of American students had become stagnant, and that we had lost ground to our international peers. College remediation rates remained high especially in subjects such as math. Some argued that the root cause was the uneven patchwork of academic standards that varied from state to state as well as a lack of agreement regarding what students should *know and be able to do* at each grade level.

As a result, it was determined that there was a need for consistent learning goals across states. In 2009, the Council of Chief State Officers (CCSSO) and the National Governors Association Center (NGA) coordinated a state-led effort to develop the *Common Core State Standards*. Designed through collaboration among teachers, school chiefs, administrators, and other experts, the standards were offered as a clear and consistent framework for educators.

The Common Core claimed to be a set of high-quality academic standards in mathematics and English language arts/literacy (ELA). These learning goals outlined what a student should know and be able to do at the end of each grade. The standards were created to ensure that all students graduate from high school with the skills and knowledge necessary to succeed in college, career, and life regardless of where they live.

The Common Core also claimed to be informed by the highest, most effective standards from states across the United States and countries around the world. These standards define the knowledge and skills students should gain throughout their K-12 education in order to graduate high school and be prepared to succeed in entry-level careers, introductory academic college courses, and workforce training programs. Overall, advocates claimed that the Common Core Standards were:

- Research and evidence based
- Clear, understandable, and consistent
- Aligned with college and career expectations
- Based on rigorous content and application of knowledge through higher-order thinking skills
- Built upon the strengths and lessons of current state standards
- Informed by other top-performing countries in order to prepare all students for success in our global economy and society.

The introduction of the Common Core was the next phase of the ongoing school reform movement resulting from the release of *A Nation at Risk* in 1983. Common Core also penetrated deeply into what had been a bedrock principle of teacher unions, the idea of academic freedom. For the first time in American education history, the national discussion regarding what students needed to learn and do was being driven mostly by *external* factors and not exclusively by educational professionals at the school, district, and state levels.

While the major teacher unions claimed to support aspects of Common Core and released statements to that effect, they argued that Common Core reduced the power of the unions to maintain control over their own professional practice. As school districts continue to adopt Common Core Standards, tensions will likely increase between administrations and unions. As of this writing forty-six states, the District of Columbia, four territories, and the Department of Defense Education Activity (DoDEA) have voluntarily adopted and are moving forward with the Common Core.

Race to the Top and Teacher Evaluation Reform

In 2009, President Barack Obama signed into law the American Recovery and Reinvestment Act, which among other things set aside roughly $4.35 billion for states to improve their education systems. The competition known as *Race to the Top* distributes funding to states that meet specific requirements and established specific plans to improve their schools.

One key area of reform as laid out by the law is teacher evaluations. The discussion of teacher evaluation reform was not new, and many school and union leaders agreed that most teacher evaluation systems were deeply flawed. Many in the public and private sector had argued for some time that current teacher evaluation models too often perpetuated mediocrity and even protected ineffective or unqualified teachers. What was new, however, was the discussion of linking teacher evaluations directly to student performance through a *value-added* model.

The idea of a value-added evaluation model and the renewed emphasis on student performance data as the most important indicator of learning sparked a whole host of reform efforts. These reform efforts subsequently led to a number of conflicts between unions, school leaders, and government officials. The list below illustrates just a few examples:

1. *2009: Michelle Rhee Launches IMPACT*: Without union negotiations, District of Columbia Public Schools Chancellor Michelle Rhee launched IMPACT, an evaluation system best known for its prioritization of value-added assessments, representing 40 percent of a teacher's evaluation. Observations conducted by "master educators," and teachers' commitment to professional development, also contributed to their final score. *Highly effective* teachers were eligible for bonuses, while *ineffective* teachers faced dismissal.

Critics of the program, particularly teachers' unions, charge that it removed experienced teachers, but many states, motivated by President Obama's Race to the Top program, have studied IMPACT while overhauling their own teacher evaluation systems.

2. *Aug. 14, 2010: Los Angeles Times Publishes Teacher Scores*: Despite resistance from teachers' unions, the Los Angeles Times published value-added scores derived from seven years of data looking at 6,000 elementary school teachers in the Los Angeles Unified School District.

   The following month, Rigoberto Ruelas, who had taught fifth grade for 14 years, committed suicide. His family blamed the publication of his "average" and "less effective" ratings for raising students' standardized test scores, and United Teachers Los Angeles urged the newspaper to remove the database from their website.

3. *Feb. 28, 2012: New York Post Reveals NYC's "Worst Teacher"*: The New York Post published the name and salary of New York City's "worst teacher" with a link to a database of value-added scores for teachers across the city.

4. *Sept. 10, 2012: Chicago Teacher Union Strike for 7 Days*: After months of heated negotiations with Chicago Mayor Rahm Emanuel, the city's teachers' union and its 26,000 members voted to go on strike, preventing more than 350,000 children from attending school.

   While wage cuts played a large role in the decision to walk out, much of the teachers' discontent stemmed from newly imposed and significantly tightened teacher evaluation requirements. The city's new REACHStudents (Recognizing Educators Advancing Chicago's Students) initiative dictated that student growth, often based on test scores, would account for 40 percent of a teacher's evaluation score, which is 10–15 percent higher than the state's requirement.

   Chicago Teachers Union president Karen Lewis estimated that the new requirements could result in the firing of 6,000 teachers, though that number has been disputed. After seven days, the union reached an agreement and called off the strike, but broader education reform issues remained.

5. *Jan. 8, 2013: Measures of Effective Teaching*: A three-year Bill and Melinda Gates Foundation study of 3,000 teachers in seven school districts, known as the Measures of Effective Teaching (MET) project, concluded that value-added scores were an accurate assessment of teachers' impact on student performance. But, noting that these assessments were even more accurate when combined with other performance measures, the study recommended that value-added scores only represent one-third to one-half of a teacher's evaluation.

The Danielson Framework for Teaching

Many states across the country have adopted the *Danielson Framework for Teaching*, a popular but controversial model for evaluation of teachers. Using a four-domain model, teachers are rated using specific rubrics and assigned a numerical rating. Most controversial for teacher unions is that in many districts, contracts are being renegotiated to include greater freedom to remove teachers who consistently receive poor evaluations under this model.

This reform is a direct response to the accusation by reformers that historically teachers unions have protected bad teachers and even prevented them from being fired. While the unions vigorously dispute this point, most school leaders will offer at least tacit agreement and stress that the removal of incompetent and ineffective teachers remains their most daunting challenge.

The Danielson Framework is still very new. Its true effect on the evaluation process and the extent to which it will help ensure a higher quality of teachers in our schools is yet to be seen. Many school leaders welcome this reform as a long overdue improvement to the current evaluation process. They argue that the new model will enhance their ability to hire and retain only the best teachers for their students. As this new value-added evaluation model becomes a reality in districts across the country, it will undoubtedly continue to heighten tensions between school leaders and unions.

Overall, these federal and state reform initiatives will continue to alter the political dynamic of union-administration relations. Demands from various aspects of society for greater accountability in schools will only increase pressure on teachers to raise student achievement, and as a result, school leaders will suffer increasing pressure to do the same. The challenge for school leaders will be to not only implement the new model, but also work closely with union leaders to minimize conflict and controversy as the model becomes a reality.

SUMMARY

In this chapter, we have discussed how unions integrate into school life, the role of their leaders and their differing styles, as well as how the reforms that are sweeping across the educational landscape are creating tensions between unions, administrations, and their leaders. More than ever before, today's school leaders will be challenged to be effective managers and competent instructional leaders. The prominence of politics in today's school leadership dynamic cannot be denied and creates a new dimension of challenge especially for new school leaders.

Unlike school leaders of the past, today's leaders will also need to be skillful politicians who can understand and embrace the art of the possible in order to meet the challenges of the new union-administration political dynamic. They will need to recognize that the politics of the union-administration relationship is one of *power sharing* and also *paradox*. While potentially frustrating to the school leader, politics and paradox are a reality in our schools, and resisting or attempting to deconstruct that relationship will only delay and damage desperately needed school reform and improvement.

The wise school leader strives to understand, embrace, and develop the relationship with the union. Leaders who want the best chance for success will strive to ensure that a sound and fair collective bargaining agreement is in place and appreciate that such an agreement will provide a common *playbook* that can serve the needs and govern the actions of both unions and administrations. Wise leaders also exhibit a strong emotional ownership of their building, staff, and students. While you never can say it out loud for fear of appearing arrogant, at the end of the day it's *your* school, *your* building, *your* students, and it's *all* your responsibility. *You* are the one "in charge."

While the role of the union is to advocate for its members and the role of the administration is to advocate for students, the art of the possible demands that both seek the common ground where the interests of both can be best served, the place where both groups can "live with" the realization of a compromise version of each other's objectives. With that in mind, the final key points in navigating the politics of unions include:

1. *Know and declare what you believe.* Form a set of core beliefs and declare what they are early. Be sure your staff and union know what you believe and what you stand for. Reflect on what you are willing to do if those beliefs are challenged. Ask yourself, what are you prepared to do? What are your nonnegotiables?
2. *Assess the culture.* Take time to watch, look, and listen to what your school culture is telling you about the state of union-administration politics. What signals are being sent? Engage in conversation with staff to glean their thoughts about union-administration relations.
3. *Know the history of union-administration politics.* What has been past practice in your school? Has there been conflict or strife between the union and administration? Was there ever a strike? If so, what *really* happened before, during, and after that strike? How many grievances have been filed in the past? What was the leadership style of your predecessor and how did it contribute, positively or negatively, to union-administration politics?
4. *Assess the balance of power.* Who really has the power? What are the symbols of that power? What does the staff think? How are decisions made? Is there a culture of accountability? Who are the "resistors" who

always oppose leader authority and change? Who are the *opinion leaders* in the building? Who does the staff look up to and respect? Who are the *"elders"*?

5. *Assess the union leader style.* Is it delegate, trustee, or combative? What is the relationship between the union leadership and your superiors?

Transformational leaders effectively manage union-administration politics and share leadership with the union and other school groups. They embrace a very important aspect of leadership: that the only thing leaders own exclusively is the *responsibility* for every aspect of the school organization, and that everything else, the credit, the celebrations of improvement and achievement, the progress, and the unrelenting determination to improve, *must be shared.*

CASE STUDY

You are a first-year high school principal, and early on, you learn that a teacher is using sick days on Mondays and Fridays to show his dogs at dog shows. You also learn that these shows are a supplementary source of income for the teacher and that the practic e has been going on for many years. After reviewing staff absence records, you confirm that this teacher is frequently absent on Mondays and Fridays and does in fact own a show dog business.

When you meet with the teacher and the building rep regarding this issue, the teacher vehemently denies the allegation. You inform the teacher that you will give him the benefit of the doubt and assume that he is being truthful. But you also direct him that if he is using sick days to show his dogs, this practice must stop. The teacher again denies any wrongdoing. For a few weeks, the pattern of absences stops but soon begins again with the absences occurring on Mondays and Fridays. Consider the following questions as you analyze this case and plan your course of action:

- Discuss how you would handle this situation? What are your next steps?
- Would you continue to investigate the situation or let it go?
- Does the fact that you are a first-year principal at this school matter?
- What do you know about the former principal and this issue?
- Will you take disciplinary action and if so what would that action be?
- How would you use your relationship with the union to help reach a positive outcome?
- What are the possible ramifications of your chosen course of action?

EXERCISES AND DISCUSSION QUESTIONS

1. Describe how you would ensure good communication with your building representative. Offer some practical examples of good communication techniques.
2. Describe how you would deal with a combative union building representative. What strategies would you use to build a good relationship?
3. As a new principal, you recognize that many grievances were filed under the past administration. Describe how you would go about assessing this situation to change this culture.
4. How would you identify the unofficial "opinion leaders" in the building? Once you do, discuss how they might help you to improve the climate and culture of your school.
5. There are a few staff members who continually oppose any change initiatives and seem intent on undermining any efforts to improve union-administration relations. What strategies would you use to manage these "resistors"?

REFERENCES

American Federation of Teachers. *History of the Common Core Standards*. (2014). Retrieved from http://www.sharemylesson.com/article.aspx?storycode=50000149.

Antonucci, M. (2015). Teachers Unions and the War Within: Making Sense of the Conflict. *Education Week. Winter*, 28–35.

Byrk, A. (2002). *Trust in Schools: A Core Resource for Improvement.* New York, Russell Sage Foundation.

Common Core Standards Initiative. (2015). Retrieved from www.corestandards.org.

Duffy, F. (2006). Power, Politics, and Ethics in School Districts: Dynamic Leadership for Systemic Change. Lanham, MD: Rowman & Littlefield Education.

Executive Summary of No Child Left Behind Act of 2001. Retrieved from https://www.google.com/webhp?sourceid=chrome-instant&ion=1&espv=2&ie=UTF-8#q=NCLB.

Giuliani, R. (2002). *Leadership.* New York: Miramax Books.

Goldstein, D. (2014). *The Teacher Wars: A History of America's most Embattled Profession.* New York: Doubleday.

Hebert, E. (2006). *The Boss of the Whole School. Effective Leadership in Action.* New York: Teachers College Press.

Loucks, H. (2005). A Teachers' Union Perspective on NCLB Accountability Issues. Retrieved from http://images.pearsonassessments.com/images/NES_Publications/2005_15Loucks_550_1.pdf.

Neff, T., and Citrin, J. (2005). *You're in Charge—Now What? The 8 Point Plan.* New York: Three Rivers Press.

Rubenstein, S. (2014). *Strengthening Partnerships: How Communication and Collaboration Contribute to School Improvement.* Retrieved from http://www.aft.org/sites/default/files/periodicals/Rubinstein.pdf.

Rubenstein, S., and McCarthy, J. (2011). Reforming Public School Systems through Sustained Union-Management Collaboration. Retrieved from https://www.americanprogress.org/issues/education/report/2011/07/13/9976/reforming-public-school-systems-through-sustained-union-management-collaboration/.

Trungpa, C. (2010). Smile at Fear: Awakening the True Heart of Bravery Boston: Shambhala Publishers.

A Nation at Risk: The Imperative for Educational Reform. Washington D.C.: The Commission on Excellence in Education, 1983. Prepared by Melissa Scherer. Retrieved from https://www3.nd.edu/~rbarger/www7/nationrs.html.

Tucker, Marc. (2012). A Different Role for Teachers Unions. Retrieved from http://educationnext.org/a-different-role-for-teachers-unions/.

Chapter 6

The Art of the Possible

Negotiating and Communicating with People

OBJECTIVES

At the conclusion of the chapter you will be able to:

1. Describe different types of communication principles and strategies (ELCC 3; InTASC 2, 7; ISLLC 3; TLEC 1, 3).
2. List and describe various tactics and counter tactics used in the negotiation process (ELCC 2, 6; InTASC 2, 7; ISLLC 3, 6; TLEC 3).
3. Describe different methods for building collaboration and teamwork (ELCC 5; InTASC 2, 7; ISLLC 3; TLEC 1, 3).
4. List and describe the major methods of effective collaborative negotiations (ELCC 3, 6; InTASC 7; ISLLC 3; TLEC 3).
5. List and describe the various methods for promoting diversity (ELCC 3; InTASC 7; ISLLC 3; TLEC 3).

THE ART OF NEGOTIATING

Negotiation is a life process. We negotiate every day from the time we wake up until the time we go to bed. We constantly negotiate with our family members, friends, and, yes, even our colleagues at work. Negotiation is an important component in ethics and politics. When people have differing political views, negotiations are a key to reaching an ethical and collaborative agreement.

Negotiation has a long and vital history in education. For example, the nation's largest education organizations are the NEA and AFT. Combined,

these associations have over four million members and their affiliate organizations are located in virtually every state. Negotiating and collective
bargaining are common processes used to reach agreement on political issues
within these organizations.

Many school districts, especially private and charter schools, do not have
union representation. However, many of these schools and districts still negotiate between employees and administration. The negotiations may be done
on a formal basis through unions or informally through faculty committees
and task forces. Regardless of the type of negotiations, there are common
principles, characteristics, and strategies used in the process.

The process of collective bargaining can be an intense negotiating process.
The process often begins with a number of activities such as:

• Reviewing of existing agreements and goals.
• Establishing the time, location, and participants to be involved.
• Establishing the roles of participants, procedures, and target dates.
• Examining past and present grievances on record by administration or
  union officials.
• Agreeing to ground rules and policies such as video or audio recording,
  press releases, and impasse procedures.

Typical negotiations involve assembling the school board team, which
might consist of the school board president, superintendent, and local school
counsel. This team might need to conduct extensive planning and preparation
including such items as financial conditions, cost analysis, bargaining issues,
work policies, roles of each member (e.g., spokespeople, observer, record-
ers), as well as negotiation ground rules. Likewise, the union representatives
would outline their ground rules and bargaining issues. Figure 6.1 lists some
typical bargaining issues between labor and management.

Informal negotiations can occur on a daily basis through the interactions
among teachers and administrators, peer groups, teachers and students, parents, community members, and politicians. Ethical and political differences
often exist among educators, and the need to work in a supportive process to
arrive to a mutual agreement should be the ultimate goal.

The negotiation process ideally should be a collaborative, win-win process.
All parties should demonstrate professional behavior and negotiate in good
faith. Some of the positive behaviors in negotiating include:

• Respecting all members and listening to their concerns.
• Controlling emotions and remaining calm.
• Taking good notes.
• Staying alert and being a good participant.

- Salary, benefits, privacy, and leave policies.

- Professional development and extra duties.

- Professional safety and security.

- Work conditions, work hours, and contract issues.

- Class size, discipline, and attendance issues.

- Impasse and grievance procedures.

Figure 6.1   Examples of school board and union bargaining issues.

- Keeping on the subject and not getting off on tangents.
- Being open-minded and cooperative.
- Avoiding premature judgments and personal distractions.

People typically have common needs when negotiating. They generally want to maintain their self-esteem and security. People generally do not like problems, surprises, feeling exploited, disrespected, loss of control, or distrust. People also can obtain a competitive edge by being well prepared, developing their negotiating skills, being knowledgeable, having high ethical standards, and taking reasonable risks.

The negotiating process can be viewed as having seven steps and characteristics as outlined in figure 6.2. The first step includes *prepare for negotiations*. In this stage, it is important to understand both your goals as well as the goals of the other party. A planning assessment might consist of determining both parties' degree of influence and power, feelings toward each other, possible concessions that might be offered, and estimated time for the process. You can never overprepare for the negotiation process, and this stage is often key to your success.

The second stage is called *humanize* the setting. Human beings are social creatures, and establishing rapport and avoiding upfront confrontations can help to support a collaborative process. Fisher and Ury in their book *Getting to Yes* refer to the collaborative process as *principled negotiations* and explain that the "goal is agreement, not victory," and that negotiators should "be soft on people and hard on the problem." They also suggest that

Figure 6.2   Steps and characteristics for the negotiating process.

in consensus building, people should "view participants as friends versus adversaries" (Fisher and Ury, 1981).

The third stage is to *initiate negotiations*. In this stage the actual process begins. Let the other party make the first offer. This usually gives you an edge in the process. You should be aware of any tactics that might be used and to be able defend against them. You might also begin by presenting the least difficult issues first in order to have a better chance of reaching agreement. This can help to build upon mutual respect and consensus, which can reinforce future agreements. Starting out with conflict generally is not a good method of building mutual agreement.

The next stage is called *collaborate on the issues*. Each of the issues is discussed and concessions are made. Concession-making is a give-and-take process. Keep track of your concessions, and try and receive something in return for every concession given. Likewise, always give yourself room to negotiate.

Give your concessions sparingly and keep track of them. Put limits on your concessions, and don't be quick to give a concession. Careful deliberation and opinions should be sought before giving up a concession, especially if a valuable one. Remember that giving a concession that costs you nothing can be an effective method of concession-making and gaining an edge in the negotiations.

Remember to maintain control of your emotions. Emotions play a significant role in the process and can help or hinder your results. Strengthen your *emotional intelligence*. Effective negotiators not only have qualities of knowledge and skills, but also are able to persuade people through their emotions. Also, be aware of the other participants' emotions, which may give you clues as to their feelings and importance of the issues.

The fifth step is called *obtain agreement*. In this stage, both parties need to be open-minded to collaboration, compromise, and accommodation when necessary to reach a satisfactory agreement. The goal is to seek mutual agreement and obtain a fair outcome, but not at the expense of the other party or yourself. If one party feels they have been exploited, they may seek reprisal, overturn the agreement, or try and get even at the next negotiations.

In the sixth stage, *close negotiations*, parties should confirm agreement on the issues. Don't talk too much during this stage, or you may evoke suspension or doubt. You might ask the other party if you have agreement, take a positive step toward closure, or read the agreement. If you see the other party express reluctance to agreement for an issue, ask what concerns the party may have. Once agreement has been confirmed, end the negotiations on a positive note, and perhaps state the next steps.

The final stage is called the *follow-up*. In this stage, follow-up steps should be agreed upon for all actions and issues. All this information should be documented, and people should be identified as accountable for follow up on the required actions. A clear and agreed-upon timetable should also be prepared. Progress meetings and follow-up status reports are recommended as well.

TACTICS AND COUNTER TACTICS

During the negotiations process, it is common practice that different *tactics* and *counter tactics* are used. A tactic is a strategy or means to gain an advantage in the negotiations process. A counter tactic is a strategy or means to defend against a tactic, and at times, gain an advantage. Figure 6.3 lists examples of negotiating tactics.

While there are many tactics that can be utilized during the negotiating process, it is important to recognize that there are just as many counter tactics

Emotional Tantrum Tactic	• Exhibiting strong emotions in an attempt to gain control over the other party.
Fait Accompli Tactic	• Presenting a final offer (accomplished fact) in an attempt to bring closure to the negotiations.
Take it or Leave it Tactic	• Making a final offer to the other party in order to close the negotiations.
Good Guy-Bad Guy Tactic	• Using a combination of a hostile negotiator and a friendly negotiator to gain a competitive advantage.
What-if Tactic	• Asking a flurry of questions in order to pry information from the other party.
Dumb is Smart, Smart is Dumb Tactic	• Asking dumb questions in order to gain information from the other party that might not otherwise be obtained.
The Expert Tactic	• Bringing in expert testimony or facts and data to convince the other party of your position.
Emotional Insulation Tactic	• Being purposely silent and not responding to create uncomfortable feelings in the other party and gain information.
The Deadlock Tactic	• Playing brinksmanship to increase the party's power and strength, and encourage concessions from the other party.

Figure 6.3   Examples of negotiation tactics and descriptions.

that can be used (Tomal, 2007). For example, if you are presented with the *if* tactic, you might counter this tactic by ignoring the statement and or using your own *what if* tactic.

The use of *fait accompli* is an attempt to bring quick closure and agreement to negotiations. However, the other party should always exercise patience and carefully examine the offer. Also, you might confront the other party as instigating a ploy to discourage this type of behavior. When faced with the *quick deal* tactic, the party should resist the tendency to give in. Likewise, you might use the *forbearance* tactic. Often, requesting additional information and being patient may allow you to discover other insightful information.

Other strategies that can help a party during negotiations include knowing the facts, figures, and information associated with the negotiation process. Also, understanding procedural laws, labor law guidelines and standards, and having total commitment for the negotiating process can give you an edge. Remember to strive to become as knowledgeable as possible about the process and bargaining issues. Also, developing your negotiating skills can help you to be more successful.

During the negotiation process, it is good to keep in mind that human beings have similar feelings, emotions, and aspirations. People generally want to be listened to, treated respectfully, given accurate information, approached in good faith, and to avoid uncertainty. Understanding these natural human feelings and behaviors can benefit the negotiator during the collective bargaining process.

The use of tactics and counter tactics in negotiating is inevitable. Recognizing a given tactic can be useful for you in selecting the most effective counter tactic. Experienced negotiators may also instinctively learn the use of counter tactics over a period of time. However, learning the names of the tactics and counter tactics and developing skills in negotiating can assist you in achieving successful outcomes.

There are many things that can go wrong during a negotiation process, especially when you are dealing with items of great importance. Not only is there a need to obtain agreement from the other party, but often the lead negotiators need to gain approval from their own constituents (e.g., school board or union members). Unfortunately, not all negotiations end amicably.

The strategy of *concession-making* can be an effective part of successful negotiations. Good negotiators always allow themselves room to negotiate. Some strategies for concession-making include:

- Ask the other party to reveal their demands first.
- Regulate and record all concession-making.
- Seek opinions prior to agreeing to a concession.
- Obtain a concession from the other party for every concession given.
- Recognize that concessions are often given at the last minute or at the deadline.

When negotiations reach an *impasse* there are often federal and state guidelines for proceeding. It is always beneficial for parties to emphasize the benefits for reaching agreement as well as the potential negative effects. In attempting to reach agreement, people can encourage settlement by discussing the details of the agreement, taking a break or changing the negotiators, and maintaining a positive attitude. Sometimes experienced negotiators might compare the current negotiating process with past negotiating sessions. In this way, the negotiator attempts to bring about consensus and agreement to the issues.

If an impasse is encountered, some of the common remedies include the use of *mediation* and *arbitration*. Mediation involves securing a mediator to act as a facilitator to broker agreement between the two parties. Generally, this process is not binding and is only an attempt to persuade each party to resolve the bargaining issues. Arbitration is similar to mediation but generally involves securing a third-party arbitrator who will review the overall bargaining issues and render a decision, which becomes binding.

Often when agreement is reached between the two parties, a ratification vote by the members and the board is necessary. If both parties are able to approve the agreement with their constituents, the agreement is consummated. It is not unusual for one of the parties to not achieve agreement, thus the need to go back to the bargaining table for additional rounds of negotiation. It should be noted that arbitration could be voluntary or compulsory.

Some states utilize compulsory arbitration as determined by state law. Other ways to resolve negotiation disputes are through the use of the Federal Mediation Conciliation Service (FMCS). This is an agency created by the federal government with the primary goal of promoting labor-management collaboration. The office of this agency is located in Washington, D.C., and it contains a list of many arbitrators who are available throughout the country.

COMMUNICATION STRATEGIES

Communication is an essential requirement of all successful negotiations. Communication can be viewed as the process of formulating information and encoding this information, transmitting the information to the receiver, decoding the information, and then providing feedback to the original transmitter. Feedback is important because it establishes and determines the quality of communication. This process can often occur almost instantaneously on a continuous basis between two people (Tomal, 2007).

Several *barriers* can impact the quality of communication. For example, the period of time when a person decides to talk to another (i.e., timing of information), the environment in which the conversation takes place, the personal approach utilized, the method or medium used, the actual selection of words, and the content all play an important part in the process.

For example, if a teacher is emotionally upset in front of other teachers, the school leader might select another time in which to confront the situation. Confronting the situation in this potentially volatile situation may embarrass the teacher and escalate the matter. The school leader may decide that the best time to address the problem might be after school when they can be alone and the teacher had time to calm down.

The *environment* plays an important part in the interactions of people. If an employee is requested by a school leader to discuss a performance issue in a formal setting, a higher degree of stress and importance may be established than in a more neutral location such as a cafeteria. If a school leader would like to address a performance issue on a more informal basis, it may be more effective to select a more neutral location.

The *medium* that is used (i.e., method of communication), such as whether a school leader uses a letter, one-on-one verbal discussion, telephone, or another person, effects the communication outcome. All these considerations should be taken into account by a school leader in deciding upon the best communication approach to use in communicating with people.

Listening is another element of the communication process. Without *active listening* on the part of both people, the communication process will be hindered. The school leader must ensure that he or she is genuinely listening to the person's position and must also ensure that the person is listening as well.

Most people speak around 150 words per minute, although they are able to listen between 400 to 600 words per minute. With this mind, a listener's mind tends to wander, and he or she begins to think about other things while listening to a speaker. It is important that both parties pay close attention to each other. For example, the school leader may request a teacher's full attention before initiating a discussion.

There are many barriers to effective listening such as interrupting the other speaker, or failing to look at the other person when talking. Also, such barriers as not allowing the other person a chance to talk, continually fidgeting with a pencil, and pacing back and forth, which are annoying behaviors, may impede effective listening. Staring at the other person, continuing to wander off the subject, attempting to finish the other person's sentences, arguing with every point, or answering a question with a question can also hinder effective listening.

Poor listeners often prejudge other individuals, daydream while listening, become bored, look uninterested, and forget the information. However, good listeners look for areas of mutual agreement, keep an open mind, listen wholeheartedly, stay awake, and give good eye contact.

For example, when a school leader is interacting with a teacher, there could be a tendency for the school leader to make preconceived notions about the teacher. The school leader might prejudge the teacher and develop a prejudice based upon past experiences. The school leader may not be open to genuinely listening to the teacher's point of view. This should be avoided to ensure effective communications.

Effective Nonverbal Communications Strategies

The use of *nonverbal communication* is also an important component in discussing a political or ethical issue with a person. Many factors impact nonverbal communication, such as proxemics, kinesics, and a person's body language.

Proxemics is the process how people use space as an extension of interpersonal communications. Some of the elements that impact proxemics include the arrangement of furniture, physical distance between two people, and the size and shape of a room. Position the furniture and setting in a more circular arrangement to support a collaborative environment.

For example, the distance between a school leader and teacher can impact the interpersonal relations during communications. A distance of more than four feet between people creates an impersonal atmosphere. A personal distance is generally about two-to-four feet between the two people. A distance of less than two feet tends to create an intimate or intimidating atmosphere.

While a person needs to consider these proxemic examples, cultural differences vary among people and need to be considered. For example, some cultures may have different degrees of eye contact, distances between people, types of handshakes, degrees of physical touching, and use of the right hand instead of the left hand when giving a person something.

Kinesics entails the study of body movements—postures, facial expressions, and gestures. People who exhibit power may use more stern gestures and direct eye contact. A more collaborative approach includes a relaxed posture, positive facial expressions, and open body gestures. While some people may attempt to exhibit intimidating body language, this probably has a negative impact on resolving a political matter and reaching mutual agreement.

People should also be aware of exhibiting defensive body language such as darting or glancing side to side, crossing one's arms in a rigid manner, or tensing body motions. These behaviors can distract the person from discussing the political issue. Positive body language can also help to support the verbal message and resolve the issues.

Effective Verbal Communication Techniques

There are several communication techniques that can be used when talking with a person. For example, you might utilize the technique of paraphrasing. *Paraphrasing* means to repeat back to the person in the person's own words what the person said. This helps to reinforce the point that an individual is listening to the person and ensure that the message is being understood.

The use of *restatement* is a technique that can be used. Restatement occurs when you repeat verbatim the other person's statement in an effort to encourage the person to continue talking. This technique can be especially effective when helping someone clarify an issue and understanding the real intent of the person.

You can use the techniques of *open-ended and closed-ended questions.* Open-ended questions cannot be answered by a simple yes or no and tend to encourage the person to continue talking. Open-ended questions usually involve words such as who, what, where, when, and how. The use of open-ended questions encourages the seeking of additional facts and information. Closed-ended questions can be effectively used when a person simply wants to obtain a yes or no answer. A simple phrase can yield a great bit of information and expedite the discussion.

Silence can be a very powerful technique when talking between two parties. Often when faced with silence, people will talk. Using moments of silence in a skillful manner can be an effective tool for opening up discussion and receiving more information from the person. Silence can also demonstrate that people are generally willing to listen to a person's concern.

The use of *expanders* is a technique of stating simple comments such as "Go on," "I understand," "I see." Expanders encourage the person to continue talking and have a reinforcing effect in establishing a mutual dialogue. A final technique includes the use of eliminating distractions within the room. A noisy environment hinders effective discussion. Finding a more suitable environment is critical in resolving political issues.

The overall goal of communications is to obtain a collaborative agreement in which both parties are satisfied. Do not feel that the negotiation element is a contest of will, that participants are adversaries, or that the goal is to make threats and demand concessions. All educators should maintain high ethical standards and employ these basic principles:

Commitment—Educators should be totally committed to the mutual process in resolving political issues. The overall focus should be on students and their learning. Commitment to students can help provide a foundation from which to negotiate political issues.

Collaboration—Educators who take a position that the feelings and opinions of people are valued and that negotiation is a two-way street will ultimately be more effective in developing trust and respect from the person. A collaborative approach in dealing with people can increase your effectiveness in achieving mutually acceptable outcomes.

Well-Defined Expectations—Nothing can undermine an educator's effectiveness as much as having ill-defined performance expectations. The expectations should be very clear, understandable, and fair for all employees.

Skill Development—Educators who continually develop their skills in the negotiating process will be more effective. The values and interests of people are often different. Your ability to work with people from different cultural and diverse backgrounds can make you an effective negotiator.

High Aspiration Level—Educators who have a high aspiration for employee and student performance are more effective in achieving meaningful goals. Educators who do not place much emphasis on high performance often create a culture of mediocrity. People generally can recognize and appreciate school leaders who embrace high-performance expectations.

Decisiveness—All educators, especially school leaders, who deal with political issues decisively will be more effective in managing the school. Letting people be apathetic, or failing to address an issue in a timely manner, can only lead to more serious problems in the school (Tomal, 2007).

BUILDING COLLABORATION AND TEAMWORK

Collaboration and teamwork are critical synergistic dispositions in reaching political agreement. *Proactive* leadership suggests the school leader's ability to anticipate the needs of employees and to take initiative in getting results. A school leader's ability to be proactive versus reactive is directly related to success in reaching collaborative agreement.

Reactive school leaders are content with the status quo and do not have the foresight to anticipate employee needs. They tend to create a working environment that is not vibrant and resourceful. Proactive leaders are often people who are service oriented. They recognize their role as being responsive to the needs of others and the organization.

The notion of servant leadership is a moral value that entails a disposition of giving and altruism. The assumption that the school leader is serving the needs of others is a key feature of ethical leadership. The concept of moral leadership encourages learning that is based on moral and societal redeeming values and goals.

One of the important aspects in reaching political agreement is the school leader's ability to manage conflict. School leaders often have employees coming into their offices with complaints and conflicts with other employees. The school leader's ability to effectively manage conflict has a direct relationship with the motivation of employees.

There are several sources of conflict in schools. Conflict can result from poor communication, roles, territorial issues, goal incongruence, stress, poor procedures and policies, and ineffective leadership. The ability of a school leader to identify the source of conflict can be an effective first step in resolving the conflict.

The perception of or actual favoritism given to employees by school leaders can be a demotivating factor. This perceived or real favoritism is a form of preferential treatment in the eyes of the employee and can lead to disciplinary or performance issues. School leaders often are unaware of the perceived favoritism they may be giving to employees.

Favoritism, or the perception of it, can be as subtle as a mere lack of prolonged eye contact or the inflection of the school leader's voice to certain staff members. For example, a school leader may be more enthusiastic and positive to some people, which can be perceived as favoritism in the view of others. Therefore, be aware of your communication and nonverbal behaviors toward all people and ensure that there is consistency and uniformity.

The personality differences among people can also be a source of conflict. Employees' personalities are often different and cause people to have varying viewpoints for a given situation. There are primarily four personality styles: *intuitors*, *feelers*, *thinkers*, and *doers*. *Intuitors* are creative and imaginative. *Feelers* tend to be sensitive and people oriented. *Thinkers* tend to be organized and methodical. And *doers* tend to be spirited and action oriented. Unlike styles among people may cause conflict.

For example, if a thinker employee is working on a project with a doer employee, the doer may be viewed as being too aggressive and short-minded. At the same time, thinkers may be seen as people who are overly logical and structured. This can frustrate people who have a different personality style.

When the feeler employee works with the doer, conflict can result. The feeler may perceive the doer's personality as being insensitive. And the feeler may be viewed as being too emotional. Likewise, others might view an intuitor as being too unrealistic and impractical. Understanding these personality styles can help in preventing and managing conflict in the workplace.

All educators are constantly involved in school change to meet requirements of state and federal regulations and improve learning. In addition, demands are often imposed on educators by parents, community members, school board members, and students. These demands, along with the need to constantly change, can cause stress and conflict. Managing change and adapting to change is a critical factor to employees. Stability can be the enemy of survival. Change is inevitable, and those who fail to effectively manage change can experience negative consequences.

The school environment can also contribute to conflict. If there is a great deal of noise and stimuli, employees may not adapt well to this environment and conflict may result. The work conditions may be distracting to an employee, and his or her ability to focus on work can be hampered. An employee also may be impacted if the temperature environment is compromised. For example, if the temperature is either too hot or too cold, employees may have a difficult time focusing on work and begin to displace negative feelings to others.

One of the contributors of conflict is that of miscommunication among people. Human beings often seek social interaction and need to communicate on a daily basis. Each of their interactions often involves a negotiating element, which leaves room for miscommunication to take place. For example, if a school leader makes a statement to an employee, and it is misunderstood, both parties may have ill feelings toward the other.

Likewise, miscommunication can take place among school leaders. There are many forms of communication such as written, verbal, and nonverbal, which impact a school leader's understanding of rules, regulations, and policies. For example, if work policies and procedures are communicated to employees and misunderstood, this may have a negative effect upon the persons' morale and performance. As a result, conflict can be generated.

One of the most significant factors impacting miscommunication is that of the grapevine communication network. There is an informal communication system called the grapevine in schools in which rumors start and contribute to misunderstandings and miscommunication (Tomal and Schilling, 2013).

Some strategies to help school leaders resolve conflict include:

• Understand the root cause and context of the conflict.
• Help people understand that there is more than one viewpoint on a matter.
• Negotiate collaboratively with the parties by examining areas of agreement and disagreement.
• Focus on the conflict issues and avoid attacking the person or becoming emotional.
• Be an active listener and maintain high ethical standards.

DIVERSITY IN THE NEW DEMOGRAPHIC

Our schools are a reflection of the diversity of our global society. There are many different terms used for diversity—pluralism, multiculturalism, or individual differences. Diversity provides organizations with interpersonal relationship challenges, as well as more opportunities for synergistic skills, viewpoints, and creativity.

Diversity in schools consists of people who have individual differences. These individual differences include age, gender, socioeconomic factors, culture, religion, ethnicity, race, family, sexual orientation, physical abilities, national origin, color, and health condition. Appreciating and building upon these individual differences can allow learning organizations to grow and contribute to high morale and student learning.

Much of our individual differences have been determined by our past values. Our values have been programmed by many different factors in our life such as schools, friends, geography, religion, family, neighborhood, media, and music. The programming messages we receive as we are growing up influence how we view people who are different from us—economically, physically, racially, spiritually, etc.

How we relate to people who are different than us is called interpersonal relations. We may have varying degrees of prejudice and favoritism because of our value differences. As a result, we may unfairly make assumptions about peoples' performance based upon their ethnicity, race, or gender. These assumptions can lead to conflict and discrimination.

As an outgrowth of the civil rights movement of the 1960s, the EEOC was established by Title VII of the 1964 Civil Rights Act to help protect diversity and enforce anti-discrimination. The original act prohibited discrimination on the basis of race, color, national origin, and gender. This law covered all aspects of employment including planning, hiring, supervising, compensation, job classification, promotions, training, and retirement and termination.

While the Civil Rights Act primarily covered all employers and public and private institutions with fifteen or more employees, the act provided the basis for bringing litigation against institutions that practiced discriminatory acts. This federal law created protected classes of employees, which mainly

Table 6.1 Examples of federal and EEOC laws and executive orders

Law	Basic Description
Title VII of the Civil Rights Act of 1964 as amended	Prohibits discrimination on the basis of race, color, gender, religion, national origin, pregnancy, childbirth, retaliation.
Pregnancy Discrimination Act of 1978	Provides protections to ensure pregnant women and new mothers are treated like any other employee with a disability.
Family and Medical Leave Act (FMLA) of 1993	Provides employees up to 12 weeks a year in unpaid leave for qualified medical and family illness, military, foster care, pregnancy, adoption, or personal serious illness.
Title VII, Section 1604, Sexual Harassment Act	Prohibits unwelcome sexual advances, requests for sexual favors, and other verbal or physical conduct of a sexual nature that creates a hostile or offensive work environment.
Age Discrimination in Employment Act 1967 (ADEA)	Protects people who are 40 or older from age discrimination or retaliation for filing a complaint.
Title I Americans with Disabilities Act of 1990 (ADA)	Protects disabled people from employment discrimination or retaliation for filing a complaint.

Source: U.S. EEOC, www.gov/laws, 2011.

consisted of women, African Americans, Asians, Hispanics, Indians, and Eskimos.

Subsequently, amendments have been made to the act which included protecting individuals above 40, disabled people, and pregnant women. Also, in 1978, the EEOC adopted other guidelines to protect claims of reverse discrimination practices as an outgrowth of affirmative action. Essentially, the act stated that organizations should avoid selection policies that have an adverse impact on hiring or employment opportunities because of race, gender, or ethnicity unless there is an organizational necessity for the practice.

The Pregnancy Discrimination Act of 1978 provides protection for pregnant women and new mothers that they be treated like people with disability for employment matters. This act was an amendment to the Title VII Civil Rights Act and impacts organizations with at least fifteen employees. This law would provide protection for pregnant women in hiring, promotion, and terminating practices.

The Family and Medical Leave Act of 1993 (FMLA) prohibits discrimination to male and female employees who desire to take 12 weeks of unpaid leave because of the birth of a child, adoption or foster care of a child, or caring for a family member who has a serious health condition. This law is administered by the *Wage and Hour Division* of the U.S. Department of Labor. The law supports people who have qualified medical and family situations leaving decisions to the discretion of the employer.

Interpretation of the law is not always clear-cut, and while guidelines have been provided by the federal agency, questions regarding what medical situations qualify remain. For example, the federal FMLA does not recognize many part-time workers who desire unpaid leave, or certain employers with less than fifty employees. Also, employees who desire to take unpaid time off for illnesses of relatives or pets, personal short-term illness, or other routine medical care are generally excluded.

Other related FMLA state statutes may apply as well. For example, the State of California recognizes domestic partners and children of domestic partners. Connecticut, however, recognizes parents-in-law of civil union partners, and the State of Hawaii recognizes grandparents of employees.

The EEOC included a sexual harassment amendment in 1980 to the Title VII Civil Rights Act. This law prohibits *sexual harassment* in the workplace. The law states that sexual harassment involves "Unwelcome sexual advances, requests for sexual favors, and other verbal or physical conduct of a sexual nature—when such conduct has the purpose or effect of unreasonably interfering with an individual's work performance or creating an intimidating, hostile or offensive working environment" (U.S. Equal Employment Opportunity Commission, 2014).

There are several types of sexual harassment discrimination in this amendment. *Adverse impact discrimination* involves the unintentional actions that have negative or detrimental effects against a person or group of people. This discrimination might involve requiring certain height requirements that could unintentionally discriminate against people of a certain ethnicity.

Adverse treatment discrimination involves the intentional act of treating people differently. An example of this discrimination could be asking different interview questions for men and women during an employment interview. *Retaliation* is an intentional discrimination when an employer commits an adverse action against the employee because he or she has complained against discrimination or filed a discrimination claim.

Another type of sexual discrimination is called *quid pro quo* (this for that, or in exchange for). This harassment is in the form of requests for sexual favors in exchange for some type of employment benefit. An example of *quid pro quo* might be a school leader requesting sexual favors from a teacher in exchange for a good performance rating or promotion.

A type of sexual harassment discrimination that is related to *environmental sexual harassment* is called *hostile working environment*. This type of harassment involves unreasonable actions that have a sexual basis that interfere with an employee's work performance. Examples might include verbal, physical, and visual sexual actions, patently offensive conduct, harassment of individuals because of their gender, displaying inappropriate sexual pictures, physically touching people, or sending sexually based content via emails.

The Age Discrimination in Employment Act (ADEA) of 1967 was designed to prohibit age discrimination for employees over 40 years of age in planning, recruiting, selection, training, promoting, transferring, compensating, and other practices of employment. The intention of the law is to prevent companies from discharging or refusing to hire older workers based upon their age. In 1986 this act was amended to prohibit discrimination in retirement for people above 40 years of age.

An example of this law would include a school district that forced a competent 60-year-old teacher to retire against his or her will in order to hire a 22-year-old teacher in order to save money for the school district. It should be noted that this law protects people who are 40 years of age or older but does not protect people who are under the age of 40.

It is never a good practice to hire or fire people based upon age rather than performance factors and needs of the school. Also, because of this law many school districts have offered early retirement programs in an effort to encourage retirement and reduce costs.

The Americans with Disabilities Act of 1990 (ADA) Title I was established to prevent discrimination against disabled individuals who can perform the essential functions of a job with reasonable accommodations. This law generally applies to employers who have fifty or more employees.

This law has had significant impact on school districts given that it covers such a wide range of medical conditions such as HIV, mental illnesses, learning disabilities, alcohol and drug addiction, and other physical ailments. This law is executed under EEOC and was subsequently amended to prohibit school districts from discrimination regardless of the number of employees.

However, an institution can claim a *bona fide occupational qualification* (BFOQ) criterion, which can be legally used to practice certain discrimination. The institution generally must show that the discrimination is essential for the direct and material impact on job performance or outcome. An example might include requiring that an individual be a Christian as a condition for employment in a Christian organization, or needing an airline pilot to meet high visual standards to fly the plane and discriminating against visually impaired people.

The penalties associated with Civil Rights Act violations can be severe. The law allows individuals who have been discriminated against to seek compensatory and punitive damages for both willful and intentional discrimination acts. Compensatory damages generally involve harm to an employee for pain and emotional suffering. Punitive damages can be assessed against an employer, which serves as punishment and a deterrent for others. There are some limitations for judgment awards depending upon the size of an organization.

SUMMARY

All school leaders should be responsible for building communications, collaboration, and trust among employees and students. School leaders need to understand the principles, strategies, and current laws and policies in managing diverse workforces. Moreover, the ability to effectively manage and resolve conflicts, and maintain high ethical standards and positive work environment is crucial for effectively operating the school.

The job of a school leader is not one to be taken lightly. School leaders need to use effective verbal, nonverbal, listening, and written communications. Also, negotiating with people to resolve ethical and political issues requires a disciplined and collaborative approach. Building respect and interpersonal communications can be an effective process to school improvement.

CASE STUDY

You are a principal at Johnson School District and have been charged with building interpersonal relations between the school board and union. The last two negotiations between the school board and union created significant conflict among the parties. For example, there were very diverse political ideologies between the two parties. The school board members believed there must be a balanced budget, fiscal conservatism, and no tax increases for community property owners. As a result, they supported a hiring freeze and larger class sizes.

The union, however, felt the district should borrow money and lobby to pass referendums to raise money to pay for smaller class sizes and creation of a school within a school. Describe how you would go about building interpersonal relations between the parties and the strategies you would use.

EXERCISES AND DISCUSSION QUESTIONS

1. List different communication strategies and how to promote effective interpersonal communications in the workplace. Also, describe some effective listening strategies.
2. Diversity principles and equal employment laws have impacted employment practices in almost all organizations in the United States. Discuss the ramifications of these principles and laws on promoting diversity, respect, teamwork, and ethics and politics in schools. Also, list some good and bad effects of these laws.
3. List different techniques for building collaboration and trust in the workplace.
4. Describe the process of negotiations to include various tactics and counter tactics in reaching political agreements in the workplace. Also, describe how ethics plays a part in the negotiation process.

REFERENCES

Tomal, D. (2007). *Challenging Students to Learn*. Lanham, MD: Rowman & Littlefield Education.

Tomal, D., and Schilling, C. (2013). *Managing Human Resources and Collective Bargaining*. Lanham, MD: Rowman & Littlefield Education.

United States Equal Employment Opportunity Commission. www.eeoc.gov/laws,2014.

Ury, L., and Fisher, R., (1981). *Getting to Yes: Negotiating without Giving in*. New York: Penguin.

Chapter 7

Ethics and Politics Case Studies

OBJECTIVES

At the conclusion of the chapter you will be able to:

1. Analyze and respond to in-depth case studies on ethics and politics related to human resource issues (ELCC 1, 2, 3, 4, 5, 6; InTASC 1, 3, 6, 9, 10; ISLLC 1, 2, 3, 4, 5, 6; TLEC 1, 2, 3).
2. Analyze and respond to in-depth case studies on ethics and politics related to school districts and boards of education (ELCC 1, 2, 3, 4, 5, 6; InTASC 1, 3, 6, 9, 10; ISLLC 1, 2, 3, 4, 5, 6; TLEC 1, 2, 3).
3. Analyze and respond to in-depth case studies on ethics and politics related to districts and unions (ELCC 1, 2, 3, 4, 5, 6; InTASC 6, 9; ISLLC 1, 2, 3, 4, 5, 6; TLEC 1, 2, 3, 6, 7).
4. Analyze and respond to in-depth case studies on ethics and politics related to financial management (ELCC 1, 2, 3, 4, 5, 6; InTASC 6, 9; ISLLC 1, 2, 3, 4, 5, 6; TLEC 1, 2, 3, 6, 7).

PRACTICE CASE STUDIES

The following comprehensive cases have been written for you as a capstone to the previous chapters of the book. They are designed to provide you with an opportunity to analyze and respond to a set of realistic and challenging cases involving ethics and politics in school districts. Good luck on your analyses of these cases and your career in school leadership.

HUMAN RESOURCES: ETHICS AND POLITICS

Case #1. "The Case of Conflict and Deceit"

You are the director of human resources of Townes School District. Townes is a city in the Midwest with just under 40,000 residents. You have just come back from vacation and find a message on your desk that is marked "urgent." The message is from a man named Mr. Heron. You call Mr. Heron and he informs you that Dr. John Blackey, the district curriculum coordinator, is the owner of Outcome Dynamics. Outcome Dynamics is the company that is presently managing the summer school enrichment program for the district.

When the phone conversation ends, you go to locate the file with last year's school board meeting minutes. After finding the file, you review minutes from the December meeting. The minutes clearly show that "Dr. Blackey replied no when asked if he had any personal connections with the Outcome Dynamics Company."

You hired Dr. John Blackey two years ago. Prior to that time, Dr. Blackey was the reading coordinator of Knoxville School District. Knoxville is a smaller district in your state. Dr. Blackey was highly recommended by the superintendent of his school district, who informed you that reading test results on the state test increased 21 percent over the six-year span in which Dr. Blackey was the reading coordinator for the Knoxville School District.

The majority of the Townes School District and community stakeholders hold Dr. Blackey in high esteem. He is perceived as a hands-on leader who likes to get personally involved with district issues. Importantly, he has received high praises for his work from families and community stakeholders. Board members value his performances as well. Importantly, he is well liked and respected by the superintendent and administrative staff in the Townes School District.

Townes School District has a diverse student population. Most of the families come from lower middle-class homes. Only 23 percent of the graduates enroll in four-year institutions of higher education. Parents in the community want to see change. They have asked the board and the school administration to provide programs and services that will positively impact the education and futures of their children. Many of their children are enrolled in the summer enrichment program that is managed by Outcome Dynamics.

In recent years, Townes School District has made progress toward improving student outcomes in the district. The district's graduation rate rose to 66 percent. This was a 14-point increase over a span of five years. Test results on the statewide test indicated an increase of about 18 percent in reading and math proficiency rates during the same five-year period.

The district formed a strategic planning committee last fall. The superintendent charged the committee with developing a strategic plan for a summer reading enrichment program. The committee consisted of Dr. Blackey, three other district administrators, four teachers, two parents, and two students. The superintendent asked the committee to send the proposal to his office within three weeks.

Members of the strategic planning committee sent the proposed recommendations to the superintendent's office within the three-week deadline. The superintendent presented the plan to the school board during the next board meeting. The superintendent followed Dr. Blackey's recommendation to use a company called Outcome Dynamics to manage the program. The total cost of the summer enrichment program to the district would be $96,000. The district followed Dr. Blackey's recommendation and voted unanimously to hire Outcome Dynamics.

Because the cost for the summer program was less than $100,000, the district was not required to hold open bidding or seek approval from the state. Board members awarded the $96,000 contract to Outcome Dynamics. The board members were confident in Dr. Blackey's recommendation.

The district sent the offer to provide summer school enrichment services to Outcome Dynamics. The company agreed to provide the services. A contract was issued and signed within two weeks. Outcome Dynamics has been managing the summer school enrichment programs for four weeks.

Exercises and Questions

1. How would you substantiate Mr. Heron's claim? What would you do if the claim is valid?
2. How could this situation have been avoided? What would be the ethical and legal implications for you as human resource director? What would be the ethical and legal implications for the superintendent of schools?
3. Research your state and district codes of ethics concerning conflict of interest by school personnel? What would be the legal implications for Dr. Blackey? Describe and discuss them in relationship to Dr. Blackey and the school district.
4. Discuss the superintendent's responsibilities related to hiring outside contractors. Did the school board members have all of the information they needed when they voted on the recommendation to hire Outcome Dynamics?
5. What are the district's professional obligations to the community? Discuss this in terms of the summer enrichment program. Should the district allow Outcome Dynamics to continue managing the summer program? Why, or why not?

Case #2. "The Case of the Superintendent's Demand"

You are the human resource manager of Dodge School District and have been informed by the district's business manager that he will be leaving the district in two weeks. You call the superintendent, Dr. Thomas, to inform him of the resignation. You remind him that the position would need to be filled as soon as possible. State auditors were to begin the financial auditing of the district in six weeks.

Dr. Thomas calls you back within two hours and informs you that he has a candidate to fill the business manager's position. He then informs you that he wants to hire Dr. Sari as the Dodge School District business manager. He further requires that you post the vacancy immediately. His aim is for Dr. Sari to begin working as soon as the business manager leaves.

After the conversation, you recall that Dr. Sari was fired from an adjacent school district five years ago for embezzling funds from student accounts. The information had been in the local news for several months that year. The news reports disclosed that Dr. Sari had embezzled funds amounting to $42,000 from the district. Newspapers and television stations also reported about the many complaints that came from district stakeholders regarding the issue.

For instance, it was reported that teachers and other district stakeholders felt that the embezzlement of funds by him betrayed the district and its students. It was also reported that many staff members of the district were seeking employment in other districts. Further, it was reported that many of the district stakeholders asked the district to pursue legal actions against him. Significantly, the district stakeholders felt that the superintendent did not handle the situation in the best interest of the students.

You make another call to Dr. Thomas to remind him of Dr. Sari's past situation. Dr. Thomas quickly replies that Dr. Sari repaid the school district for the entire sum of money. He reminds you that the former district did not file legal charges against him. He then informs you that he was an excellent business manager and would be an asset to Dodge School District. Further, he reminds you that he is the "one in charge" and you are to follow his directives.

Dodge is a small school district of less than 700 students and 100 employees. The diverse groups of students are housed in three buildings, an elementary school, the middle school, and the high school. Based on the free lunch applications, 98 percent of the students in the district qualified for free or reduced lunch. Notwithstanding, about 55 percent of the students go on to postsecondary education, usually the community college or state universities.

You feel that your position as the Dodge School human resource manager obligates you to make every effort to select individuals on the basis of competency and character. You do not feel that Dr. Sari has the character that is needed to perform the duties of a district business manager. Further, you feel that hiring him would not align with the ethical standards of Dodge School District in relationship to trust and honesty.

You spend the rest of the day working with your administrative assistant. By the end of the day, you have posted the vacancy. You then sit and ponder the situation.

Exercises and Questions

1. What would be your next step? Discuss your answer in relationship to the Dodge School District Board of Education, your responsibilities as the human resource manager, and the ethical principles embedded in the case.
2. Research information relating to district professional standards and superintendent responsibilities. What is the primary problem in this case? What are the secondary problems in the case?
3. Research the educator codes of ethics in your state and district. What are the obligations of districts in regard to hiring district personnel? Find specific ethical standards relating to the issues in this case. Discuss them in relationship to your role as human resource manager.
4. What do you think would happen if Dr. Sari was hired? How do you think the district staff would react? How do you think the community would react?
5. Define the terms values, ethical standards, and leader. Summarize those terms as they define Dr. Thomas and his actions.

DISTRICTS AND BOARDS: ETHICS AND POLITICS

Case #3. "The Case of the Faulty Realignment Plan"

You are the superintendent of a large suburban high school district comprised of three high schools. Your district belongs to the Southwest Interscholastic Athletic Association (SIAA), a conference of twenty high school districts engaged in various athletic and interschool contests and events. Your district is a founding member and has been associated with SIAA for nearly 20 years.

SIAA is governed by three boards comprised of Board 1, athletic directors, Board 2, principals, and Board 3, the district superintendents. Boards 1 and 2 are advisory, while the final decisions for all SIAA governing rules are made by the superintendent board. In recent months, you have been troubled by conversations about breaking up SIAA into smaller more manageable regional areas because it has grown so large with high schools being added to the conference, raising the student population to nearly 100,000 students.

Up to now, the conference demographics have been fairly balanced, but the distance between schools has always been a concern. In some cases, it can take students and coaches nearly an hour or more to travel for away competitions because of congested suburban traffic. The three boards are struggling with the difficult issues of 1) travel times and 2) the impact on students leaving early resulting in the loss of instructional time.

In the last superintendent meeting, the agenda contained an item on conference realignment; however, that discussion was canceled once the meeting began. You take little notice of this. Then you begin to hear rumors that several superintendents are meeting together to realign the conference and create a voting block to push the realignment through without debate. But the rumors die down and the school year ends without further action.

In the summer meeting of the superintendent board, you arrive to find standing room only in the meeting. You did not receive an agenda for the meeting but noticed one on the table. In the agenda, you find that the SIAA realignment is on the agenda for a vote to approve. You are at a loss because you have not seen a realignment plan nor has it been discussed.

When the time comes for the vote, there is a brief discussion stating that the AD and principal boards have recommended a realignment of the conference into four regions based on geographic location within the conference. As you scan the locations and the proposed regions, you realize that the east region (in which your schools have been placed) has a solid majority of schools with mostly minority students, while the other three regions have a majority of schools with mostly white students.

The vote is taken with 17 superintendents voting yes and 3 voting no. You are one of the three voting no. In your no vote, you explain to your colleagues that this plan is based on a misalignment of demographics and you want no part of it. But the plan passes anyway.

You take this news back to your board of education, who become quite angry and in the mood to fight. They write a letter of protest to every school board in SIAA outlining the racial imbalance and discriminatory realignment. There is no response from the other boards. The local press in all the communities served by SIAA covers the realignment plan and the dissent by the three district boards affected by the yes vote. The press takes on the issue and creates a "firestorm" of letters to the editors in the various communities.

The national press enters the fray with TV, radio, and print outlets covering the realignment. The press frames the situation in terms of racial discrimination and begins to interview parents, students, community members, as well as local school board members. You notice that there are innuendoes, half-truths, and outright lies being presented to the general public. You are having a difficult time managing the public relations, as well as members of your own board of education.

You decide there must be a plan of action devised for this situation, as it is rapidly escalating out of control, and your students, your communities, and your school reputations are being ruined by negative press. You decide to meet with the other two superintendents who also voted no to devise a plan of action to address the situation.

Exercises and Questions

1. Research and outline which federal and/or state statutes may influence and impact the plan of action you may take in this case.
2. What personal ethical considerations play into this case? Explain why.
3. How will you help your board of education keep their perspective and focus on what is in the best interests of your students and that of SIAA?
4. Chart a possible plan of action and response to the case. What steps will you recommend to your superintendent colleagues? How will you keep the board of education up-to-date, and what part should they play in this case?
5. Outline the possible steps in a positive public relations plan to address this case.
6. Are there any legal actions that may support your plan of action? If so, outline those possible remedies.

Case #4. "The Case of the Inappropriate Comments"

You are the superintendent of a PK-12 school district of 8000 students. You have a newly elected board. Four new members have come on board winning the election as a voting block to protest the prior board's actions as "caving in" to the union during the recent teacher contract negotiations.

You find that they are a contentious four who question every decision you make and every action taken by the previous board. You find it difficult to have a working relationship with the board. You find that they make inappropriate comments in public session and have often made derogatory comments about the previous board and union leadership. Up to now, their comments have been of a general nature and not personal.

In closed sessions, you have counseled them about the importance of keeping their public comments professional and related to the district needs and goals. You have also counseled them about their protections under the district insurance plan covering actions that pertain only to their work directly related to board meetings and district operations.

In a spring meeting, one of the four new members begins a tirade about the union demands for a fair implementation of the recently approved contract.

The union has threatened grievances if any part of the approved contract is changed or not implemented. The board member begins to call various union members by name and uses derogatory comments about each one.

Several of the newly elected board members join in this personal tirade. You lean over to your board president and ask that she call a halt to the meeting and immediately ask for a closed session meeting of the board. She does so and the board members leave to go into closed session.

In the closed session, you remind the board members of their public actions and their comments. Then you directly tell them they cannot call out individual people by name and make derogatory comments about them. They must remain professional. Further, you tell them that they are making it difficult for you to manage the district and that their insulting comments violate your own personal code of ethics. You ask them to stop. They argue with you.

You leave the meeting and go to the boardroom and ask that the school board attorney return with you to the closed session. Back in the closed session, you ask the attorney to explain in detail the legal implications for board members stepping out of their role as an elected board member and making insulting comments to members of the community and the district staff. He does so.

The board returns to open session. Once in open session, one of the four board members again steps out of bounds and begins the name-calling. The board president steps in and stops it immediately. The remainder of the board business remains calm, and the board completes their agenda without further comments.

You arrive to your office the next day to find a grievance filed on behalf of the union, as well as a phone call from an attorney representing two of the union leadership team. The union is protesting the name-calling in the grievance. The faculty union leaders are suing the district and the board of education for defamation.

Exercises and Questions

1. Research and review the laws governing the open meetings act. What actions are required for open sessions and what are required for closed sessions?
2. Research grievance procedures in your state. What statutes govern these procedures? What is the grievance procedure in your school district?
3. Research insurance coverage for boards of education. What insurance coverage protects board members in their roles as members and what are not covered? Research your district's umbrella insurance plan. What actions are covered as professional duties?

4. What personal ethical considerations are covered in this case? Explain why.
5. What action would you take to improve board working relationships?
6. What potential action could the four members take that could jeopardize your tenure as the superintendent in the district? How do you protect yourself from such jeopardy?

UNIONS: ETHICS AND POLITICS

Case #5. "The Case of the Toxic Culture"

You are a first-year principal at a large high school in a unit district with eight schools. You have a few years' experience as a school leader but not in a comprehensive high school. Your new position begins in January. The district has a very high poverty and mobility rate. There is significant gang activity in the community. Your high school has a reputation of poor academic achievement, bad student behavior, and very little accountability for faculty and staff. Even so, the superintendent tells you that the high school has always been the "flagship" of the district.

The district also has a long history of bitter union relations that has its roots in a strike occurring several years prior to your coming to the district. The strike lasted several weeks making it one of the longest teachers' strikes in state history. Some veteran staff tells you, that despite the difficulty of the strike, it brought the union members closer and seems to endure as a topic of conversation for teachers and staff. Your high school has a wall-to-wall union meaning that all employees are members of the same union.

Union leadership has a reputation for militancy and has created conditions that are very difficult for school leaders. Grievances are frequent and as a result, several school leaders have left the district. The relationship between the superintendent and the union president is especially difficult and is becoming personal and visceral since the strike.

A few years after the strike, the district was facing bankruptcy. To remedy the crisis, the state legislature created a finance authority with a ten-year charter for governance of the district. In order to set the district on a course of financial recovery, the state finance authority implemented deep budget cuts. Salaries were frozen, and budgets for athletics and extracurricular activities were dramatically reduced or eliminated completely. Academic programs and course offerings were reduced resulting in teacher layoffs. Building and grounds budgets were also greatly reduced causing your building to fall into disrepair.

As if all this was not enough, for the last few years the students of your high school have consistently scored below the Annual Yearly Progress standards established by the NCLB legislation. As a result, the school was placed on academic warning requiring you and your leadership team to write a comprehensive three-year school improvement plan.

As you enter your new position as principal, you recognize that morale and employee self-esteem in your school are very low and that there appears to be little hope or optimism that things will improve. Your building leadership team is understaffed as department chairs and other administrative positions were eliminated by budget cuts. There is little or no money or resources for school improvement, but nonetheless, the faculty, staff, and the school board are looking to you to lead them.

Exercises and Questions

1. List and describe the first steps you will take as principal to improve relations with union leaders. How will you attempt to gain an understanding of the factors that contributed to the current toxic relationship? Ask a student colleague to assist you in a role-play activity where your colleague is the union leader and you are the principal. What are the key elements of that conversation? What questions need to be asked? Since your high school has a wall-to-wall union, do you think it makes any difference or has any effect on the state of union-administration relations?

2. List and describe the questions you will ask faculty and staff regarding the state of union-administration relations. Describe what it is that you are trying to learn and understand? How will you go about determining the factors that contributed to the toxic culture of the school? List and describe your process for identifying the positive aspects of the school culture.

3. Obtain a copy of your school's current union contract along with contracts from four other school districts. Create a comparison chart of all five contracts. What are their similarities and differences? What does each of these contracts say to you about the politics of their respective schools?

4. Research the definition of a formal grievance and list the step-by-step processes. Describe, in detail, the difference between a grievance and a complaint. List and describe the formal grievance process in schools. What is your duty as a school leader regarding the formal grievance process?

Case #6. "The Case of the Broken Promise"

You are the principal of a midsize elementary school. The relationship between the union and administration is not good, not bad, but best described as benign. You have been told that the union leaders have an unusual relationship with the assistant superintendent for human resources. Members of your leadership team have shared that he has great influence on the board of education, even more than the superintendent, and that they believe he has even been complicit with union leaders in the removal of former administrators, including the former principal.

Shortly after starting as principal, you learn that an unusual item was bargained into the recently ratified agreement between the district and the union. The district agreed to allow the union to distribute a survey among their members that will solicit teacher and staff satisfaction regarding administrator performance. Administrators were not informed of this agreement until after the contract was ratified.

When administrators inquired about this agreement, the assistant superintendent for human resources promised that only the superintendent and the administrator being rated would see the results. He also indicated the results would not play any part in the evaluation of administrators, but would be used only as reflective feedback for that administrator. On more than one occasion, the assistant superintendent stressed that the union had promised to not disclose the results of the survey except to the superintendent, who would then share results with the individual administrator.

Not long after the staff completed the survey, a teacher and member of the union executive board asked to see you. At the time, he indicated that the union had openly shared the results of the survey, including individual administrator satisfaction ratings, with the entire faculty and staff at a recent union meeting. He said that he believed that this action was unprofessional and broke their promise to keep the results confidential. He said that he respected you and thought you should know. He also asked for you to keep the conversation confidential, as he was concerned that if anyone discovered that he shared this information, there might be backlash from his union colleagues.

By making some discreet inquiries, you verify that the results of the survey were, in fact, shared with the entire staff at the union meeting. In the meantime, members of your leadership team have also learned of this and are understandably upset. They are all asking you to express their outrage to the superintendent and to demand an end to the use of this survey.

Exercises and Questions

1. List and describe the aspects of this situation that you feel confident are true and those that you feel will need further investigation. Once you do, what are your next steps? What will you say and do to reassure your leadership team? Describe, in detail, your conversation with your superintendent as you work toward resolution of this issue.

2. Did the union violate the collective bargaining agreement by sharing this survey information with the entire staff? Research collective bargaining agreements from other schools, along with school labor law, to determine if the union had a contractual requirement to honor their pledge to reveal the survey results only to the superintendent. If it is determined that the union's failure to honor their pledge is not a violation of the contract, what are your next steps?
3. List and describe the key features of your conversation with the superintendent. How will you communicate the concerns of your leadership team? Will you ask that the assistant superintendent be involved in that conversation? The superintendent will either support you or he won't. What is your plan for both scenarios as they pertain to working with your leadership team going forward?
4. What are the problematic elements of this situation? Where did both sides go wrong? What could both sides have done differently? Conduct an educational literature search on union-administration relations. What are the key features of successful and productive partnerships between unions and school leaders?

FINANCE: ETHICS AND POLITICS

Case #7. "The Case of the Financial Kickbacks"

You are being offered a contract as a superintendent for a large suburban school district in southwestern United States. Unfortunately, you would be entering the position in the middle of the school year because the prior superintendent and the human resource director were abruptly terminated by the school board for unprofessional conduct and financial mismanagement. You are hesitant to take this new job instead of continuing to search for a better one because this district appears to be a mess. But you need a job, and this position should give you a chance to gain experience as a superintendent, which eventually may lead to a better position.

You are also surprised the school board is offering the position to you as you have no prior experience as a superintendent. However, you believe the position can provide some valuable experience and allow you to help the school district, especially given the abrupt departure of the former district leaders. So you decide to take this challenging position.

Upon accepting the position, the school board has made it clear that you need to clean up some major ethical and financial issues left by your predecessor. The school board is asking you to present a plan as to how you are going to address these major issues. Described below are the issues that were presented to you by the members of the school board:

1. The former superintendent apparently had given a no-bid contract to the Valley Bay Consulting Company (vendor) to purchase a new benefits and compensation system without seeking school board approval. You were told that this system is a modern, leading-edge program for tracking teacher evaluations, benefits, and payroll lane changes, as well as streamlining the payroll system. The former human resource (HR) director told the union: "We don't want to give teachers raises just because they live and breathe another year—it needs to be based upon performance." However, apparently, the former HR director's family member is owner of the consulting firm.

   The case gets more involved because a reliable staff member told you that the HR director had received several gifts in excess of $100 from the vendor. Moreover, a community member, who has inside information about the issue, indicated that the former HR director had been given a part-time consulting position with a relative of the vendor to conduct HR consulting during the summer and weekends. This community member believes that this is an indirect kickback for authorizing the new computer system, which was apparently done without school board approval.

2. Further, the situation in the district became more complicated when the school board discovered, through an independent audit, that the former superintendent mismanaged school funds. Apparently, he sought reimbursement for expenses for many dinners with vendors where alcoholic beverages were purchased. Several of these receipts were apparently fraudulent and also various teachers and staff members participated in the dinners.

3. Adding to the financial debacle, the former superintendent also apparently gave a no-bid contract to an insurance vendor to provide all the health and liability insurance for the district in exchange for a kickback estimated to be in excess of $10,000. Apparently, the money was given in cash and over several transactions. So far, however, there is no evidence of the financial transactions. A further criminal investigation into these transactions is pending.

   The school board is expecting you to follow up on these issues and to provide a detailed plan on how to address the issues.

Exercises and Questions

1. List and describe all the major state and federal laws and statutes that may have been violated in this case. Investigate what are typical local school district policies, and research your own school district policies that relate to these issues. Also, what kind of legal exposure might the school district have if the former superintendent is not charged with any crime? What

defense measures or precautions could a school district employ in these matters?

2. Describe why the conduct of the former superintendent and HR director is in direct violation of standard ethical behavior. How do you, as a district leader, ensure that candidates selected for key district leadership positions exhibit high ethical standards? Describe your hiring practices for this key character trait.

3. Develop an action plan for investigating and addressing these issues requested by the school board. Include the people who need to be involved, timeframe, and steps in approaching the issues.

4. Conduct a literature search, and identify issues similar to those in this case and how they were resolved. In addition, describe what other measures could be taken to help prevent these issues from happening in the future. Identify other school district leaders who may act as a "check and balance" for each ethical and possible criminal violation.

Case #8. "'The Case of Conflicts of Interests"

The Miller Falls School District is growing rapidly. The district is comprised of one high school, one middle school, and two elementary schools. You have been newly promoted from high school principal to assistant superintendent of curriculum and instruction. The superintendent convinced the board of education that the district needs to hire several full-time positions. The positions include a safety officer, transportation specialist, and an information technology director. The superintendent, Mr. Smith, would like to fill these positions by hiring staff members from his previous district. Two of the people are distant relatives, and the other is a very close friend of his wife's boss.

You believe that the positions are not needed and that spending money on these positions is a poor use of resources. It appears that the district is adequately serving the needs of the students without creating these new positions. You suspect that Mr. Smith wants to build his empire of administrators and exercise his power by rewarding his relatives and obtaining favor from his wife's boss.

In addition to the hiring concern, you believe that Mr. Smith appears to be sanctioning the misuse of federal Title IV funds that were recently given to the district. The funds are to be used for improving the children's reading performance; however, you suspect that the funds are not being used in the best interest of the children, but rather for political favors given by the superintendent.

You have overheard a discussion between the superintendent and a colleague where the superintendent stated, "I just want to keep the teachers happy so I don't get any flak from them. There are several influential teachers who have significant power in electing the board members and I would like to keep my job."

This statement was very disconcerting to you. You are not entirely sure if he was being totally honest or he was just making a half-hearted attempt at humor. But your suspicion is that he means exactly what he said regarding the operation of the so-called reading-improvement program. Apparently, the program only consists of an after-school program for the struggling children staffed by a select group of teachers who are being given a generous stipend to teach reading.

However, all that ever happens in the program is that the children sit and read books in a glorified study hall while the teachers are either half-sleeping in the front of the room or reading their own books to pass the time. The rumor among staff members is that the only reason the reading program exists is to provide extra income for the superintendent's cronies to make extra money at the expense of the children.

You are very troubled by this situation. You also are being hesitant, and you struggle how to approach this situation given you are new in your position and don't want to jeopardize your own job. You're afraid that if you expose the situation, you will receive the wrath of Mr. Smith. You have heard that Mr. Smith demands complete loyalty and will punish anyone who demonstrates even the slightest disloyalty.

Exercises and Questions

1. What are the ethical ramifications in this situation? What issues might be ethical concerns versus actual legal or school district policy violations? List and describe typical local school district policies, and cite your own school district policies that relate to these issues.
2. Develop an outline of how you would approach addressing this situation? What would you do if Mr. Smith began to suspect that you were questioning the quality of the Title IV reading program and the intentions of the parties involved? How do you protect yourself from political retribution?
3. Research various federal entitlement programs and typical regulations and expectations on how monies should and should not be spent. What types of documentation and deliverables do federal programs typically require?
4. In the school system where you work or reside, how are resource allocation decisions determined? Is there a process for evaluating whether resources result in increased student performance?

Appendix A

Political Activities

What Can I Do?

Generally, as a result of the 1993 amendments to the Hatch Act, federal employees may participate in political management or political campaign activities. The basic "Do's" and "Don'ts" are:

DO'S

- May be a candidate for public office in nonpartisan elections
- May register and vote as you choose
- May contribute money to political organizations and candidates
- May speak at a political gathering even a fundraiser
- May assist in voter registration drives
- May attend and be active at political rallies and meetings
- May stuff envelopes for a campaign
- May join and be an active member of a political party or club
- May sign nominating petitions
- May campaign for or against referendum questions, constitutional amendments, municipal ordinances
- May campaign for or against candidates in partisan elections
- May distribute campaign literature in partisan elections
- May hold office in political clubs or parties

DON'TS

- May not be a candidate for public office in partisan elections
- May not use official authority or influence to interfere with an election

- May not use official title in political activities
- May not collect political contributions unless both individuals are members of the same federal labor organization or employee organization and the one solicited is not a subordinate employee
- May not solicit or receive political contributions from the general public
- May not knowingly solicit or discourage the political activity of any person who has business before the department
- May not wear political buttons while on duty or in a government building
- *May not engage in political activity while on duty*
- *May not engage in political activity in any government office*
- *May not engage in political activity while using a government vehicle*
- *May not engage in political activity while wearing an official insignia*

* Italicized prohibitions do not apply to employees who are appointed by the president *and* confirmed by the Senate.

NOTES AND CAUTIONS

Under the Hatch Act, unless otherwise noted, career and noncareer employees are treated the same. However, these guidelines do not apply to career SES employees or administrative law judges whose political activities are more restricted. Any additional restrictions on *noncareer* employees would be by department policy. Check with the special assistant/White House liaison in the Office of the Secretary.

ETHICS AT A GLANCE provides general guidance. For specific information, call the Ethics Division at (202) 401-8309. Published by the U.S. Department of Education, Office of the General Counsel.

Appendix B

Outside Activities

Most employees may earn outside income and engage in outside activities, subject only to the federal conflict of interest statutes and the Standards of Ethical Conduct. Generally, employees may engage in any activities—paid or volunteer—as long as the activities do not require the employee to disqualify himself or herself from duties central to his or her position within the department.

In addition, although complicated by a recent court decision and subject to an exception for teaching certain courses—in most circumstances, employees may not accept pay (including travel reimbursement) for teaching, speaking, or writing related to the employee's duties.

Employees must obtain approval prior to:

1. providing services, other than clerical, on behalf of any other person in connection with a matter in which the United States is a party or has a direct and substantial interest, or when the provision of services involves the preparation of materials for submission to, or representation before, a federal court or executive branch agency;
2. serving as an officer, director, trustee, general partner, agent, attorney, consultant, contractor, employee, advisory committee member, or active participant for a prohibited source; or
3. teaching, speaking, writing, or consulting that relates to the employee's official duties. An exception permits employees to engage in many volunteer activities without obtaining prior approval, such as participating in:
   1. a social, fraternal, civic, or political entity;
   2. a religious organization that is not a prohibited source;

3. a PTA or similar organization at the employee's child's school or day care center, other than as a member of the board of directors or other governing board of the school or center; or
4. volunteering to tutor or provide direct social or medical services.

Under what circumstances would the department deny my request to work part-time for an outside organization?

Denials are rare, but they do happen. For example, an employee sought approval to work part-time for a nonprofit grantee of the department. The employee's duties included monitoring the performance of the grantee, *and* her supervisor indicated that it was impossible to assign this project to a coworker. The employee would be barred by law from doing her department job if she took this part-time position. Therefore, the department denied her request.

How can I tell whether a proposed outside activity is "related to my duties"? The definition includes, among other things:

1. activities undertaken as part of your official duties;
2. offers extended to you because of your official position, and not because of your expertise;
3. offers extended to you by a person or group that has interests that may be affected substantially by the performance of your duties;
4. matters dealing in significant part with any matter to which you are currently assigned or have been assigned within the past year; or
5. matters dealing in significant part with any ongoing policy, program, or operation of the department.

Why do I have to get approval before serving on the board of directors of my child's school?

In most, if not all, cases approval will be granted. However, because criminal conflict of interest statutes restrict some activities of federal employees, the approval process gives the Ethics Office an opportunity to give you advice about these restrictions. For example, as a federal employee, you may not represent the school before a federal agency (e.g., the Internal Revenue Service). Further, even though you are not paid to serve on this board, it would be a violation of a criminal law for you to participate in a particular matter at the department that has a direct and predictable effect upon the financial interests of the school. Thus, absent a waiver, you are required to disqualify yourself from both general policy and specific party matters that involve the school or affect its financial interests.

Where can I obtain a copy of the outside activity request form?

You may get a copy of the form from your executive officer or the Ethics Division.

ETHICS AT A GLANCE provides general guidance. For specific information call the Ethics Division at (202) 401-8309. Published by the U.S. Department of Education, Office of the General Counsel.

Appendix C

Gifts Between Employees

The Standards of Ethical Conduct limit gifts between employees, particularly gifts to supervisors. The general rule is: an employee may not give—or make a donation toward—a gift for his or her supervisor. An employee's supervisor includes the employee's immediate supervisor as well as any other employees who direct or evaluate the employee's performance or the performance of any of the employee's supervisory superiors.

There are three basic exceptions to this rule:

1. Employees may give—or voluntarily "chip in" for—food or refreshments to be shared in the office;
2. An employee may give a gift to his or her supervisor on an occasional basis including recurring events when gifts are traditionally exchanged, such as birthdays and holidays, as long as the gift is not cash and is worth $10 or less. Employees may not "chip in" to buy a group gift for these events; and
3. An employee may give a supervisor a gift appropriate to the occasion for special, infrequent events, such as the birth of a child or marriage, and for occasions that end the supervisory relationship, such as retirement or reassignment. For these events, employees may "chip in" to buy a group gift as long as the individual contributions are a nominal amount and entirely voluntary.

May I, as a supervisor, collect money from my staff to have an office baby shower for another employee on my staff?

The purpose of these rules is to protect employees from feeling coerced into giving gifts, while permitting some limited, voluntary social exchange between employees. Thus, supervisors may not solicit gifts from those they supervise—even if the gift is for another employee (and certainly not for themselves or another supervisor). Someone on your staff will have to take the initiative to hold this event. Of course, you may, on your own, give your employee a baby gift.

Our supervisor's birthday is coming up; what can we do to celebrate this event?

Employees may bring—or collect voluntary contributions to buy—a cake and other refreshments to share in the office for a birthday party. It is not permissible, however, for the staff to collect money and "chip in" together to buy a birthday gift, although employees individually may give the supervisor a gift valued at $10 or less. Similarly, because a group gift is impermissible for this type of recurring event, it is not proper for the group to take the supervisor to a restaurant for lunch.

Our supervisor's husband has been very ill, and was recently hospitalized; may the staff send him flowers?

An employee may directly or indirectly give a gift to a supervisor on special, infrequent occasions, such as a major illness. For these types of events, a group of employees may voluntarily "chip in" nominal money contributions (e.g., less than $10) to purchase the flower arrangement, or an employee may send flowers on his or her own.

I travel at least once a month in my job; may I bring my supervisor an inexpensive souvenir from each of these trips?

Gifts between employees and supervisors are permitted on an occasional basis, including occasions when gifts are traditionally exchanged. This is much too frequent to be considered occasional.

I'm in charge of collecting money for a retirement gift for our office's supervisor; may I tell everyone on the staff that they should contribute $4 each for this gift?

Contributions must be voluntary. Thus, although an amount may be recommended, the recommendation must also indicate that employees are free to contribute less or nothing at all.

ETHICS AT A GLANCE provides general guidance. For specific information call the Ethics Division at (202) 401-8309. Published by the U.S. Department of Education, Office of the General Counsel.

Appendix D

Code of Ethics

AASA'S STATEMENT OF ETHICS FOR EDUCATIONAL LEADERS

An educational leader's professional conduct must conform to an ethical code of behavior, and the code must set high standards for all educational leaders. The educational leader provides professional leadership across the district and also across the community. This responsibility requires the leader to maintain standards of exemplary professional conduct while recognizing that his or her actions will be viewed and appraised by the community, professional associates, and students.

The educational leader acknowledges that he or she serves the schools and community by providing equal educational opportunities to each and every child. The work of the leader must emphasize accountability and results, increased student achievement, and high expectations for each and every student.

To these ends, the educational leader subscribes to the following statements of standards.

The educational leader:

1. Makes the education and well-being of students the fundamental value of all decision-making.
2. Fulfills all professional duties with honesty and integrity and always acts in a trustworthy and responsible manner.
3. Supports the principle of due process and protects the civil and human rights of all individuals.
4. Implements local, state, and national laws.

5. Advises the school board and implements the board's policies and administrative rules and regulations.
6. Pursues appropriate measures to correct those laws, policies, and regulations that are not consistent with sound educational goals or that are not in the best interest of children.
7. Avoids using his or her position for personal gain through political, social, religious, economic, or other influences.
8. Accepts academic degrees or professional certification only from accredited institutions.
9. Maintains the standards and seeks to improve the effectiveness of the profession through research and continuing professional development.
10. Honors all contracts until fulfillment, release, or dissolution mutually agreed upon by all parties.
11. Accepts responsibility and accountability for one's own actions and behaviors.
12. Commits to serving others above self.

*used with permission from the AASA.

Index

About the Authors

Daniel R. Tomal, PhD, is Distinguished Professor of Leadership at Concordia University Chicago teaching educational leadership. He is a former high school teacher, administrator, corporate vice president, consultant, and professor. He received his BS and MAE degrees in education from Ball State University and a PhD in educational administration and supervision from Bowling Green State University. He has authored nineteen books such as *Action Research for Educators*, *Grant Writing* (with Rekha Rajan), *Resource Management for School Administrators* (with Craig Schilling), *Managing Human Resources and Collective Bargaining* (with Craig Schilling), *Leading School Change: Maximizing Resources for School Improvement* (with Craig Schilling and Margaret Trybus), and *The Teacher Leader* (with Craig Schilling and Robert Wilhite). He has made a guest appearance on many national radio and television shows.

Robert K. Wilhite, EdD, is professor of leadership at Concordia University Chicago and chair of the Department of Educational Leadership. He received a BA in humanities from Southern Illinois University, Edwardsville, a MA in reading and learning disabilities, and an EdD in curriculum, instruction, and administration from Loyola University Chicago. He is a former high school English teacher; elementary, middle school, and high school principal; associate superintendent for curriculum and instruction; and superintendent of schools. He is coauthor of several books including *The Teacher Leader* and *Supervision and Evaluation for Learning and Growth*. He has made numerous presentations at conferences in areas of leadership styles, curriculum development, school improvement, and change processes. He also currently serves on the Illinois Licensure Board, Principal Review Panel, evaluating the design of university principal preparation programs.

Brenda F. Graham, EdD, is professor of leadership at Concordia University Chicago. She is a former high school science teacher, school principal, and superintendent of schools. She received a BA degree in biology from the University of Arkansas in Pine Bluff, an MS degree in biology from Chicago State University, and an EdD in educational leadership and administration from the University of Arkansas in Little Rock. She has written many articles and made numerous presentations at conferences in the areas of assessment, accountability, and diverse learning practices. She also provides consulting services to clients in the areas of school improvement, strategic planning, violence prevention, human resource management, and program planning.

Jeffrey T. Brierton, PhD, is associate professor of leadership at Concordia University Chicago. He is a former teacher, union president, and high school principal who received a BA degree in political science from Elmhurst College, an MA degree in political science from Roosevelt University, a MSEd from Northern Illinois University, an EdS from National Louis University, and a PhD in American History from Loyola University. He teaches leadership courses and is a university supervisor for the CUC principal internship program. He is also a retired ten-year veteran of the U.S. Army Reserve.